Chakras

The Definitive Handbook For Novices On Unveiling The Third Eye, Engaging In Mindfulness Practices, And Exploring The Potency Of Crystal Therapy

(An Introductory Guide To Chakra Healing For Novices)

Duncan Davies

TABLE OF CONTENT

Restoring Equilibrium To The Sacral Chakra.............. 1

Healing The Fourth Chakra.. 9

Chakra And Relationships 21

Ensuring Equilibrium In Your Day-To-Day Existence 36

Sacral Chakra Meditations 62

Engaging In A Meditative Practice For The Sacral Chakra: "Invocation Of Vom" 91

Opening Your Chakras 93

Attaining Chakra Healing And Activation Via Simplified And Pragmatic Measures 112

Achieving Chakra Healing Via The Practice Of Mindful Existence 149

Restoring Equilibrium To The Sacral Chakra

The second of the seven primary chakras is known as the sacral chakra, identified as 'swadhisthana' in the Sanskrit language. The hue exhibited by the object in question is a shade of orange, symbolizing its association with the water element. It possesses the subsequent symbol.

What is the Function of the Sacral Chakra?
The sacral chakra is located superiorly to the pubic symphysis and inferiorly to the umbilicus. It assumes responsibility for governing your artistic and procreative abilities, as well as fostering a profound sense of self-fulfillment and emotional contentment. It pertains to your sexual desire, governing and managing any associated issues relevant to it. The sacral chakra also governs the extent of your inspiration and motivation, your capacity to foster

emotional bonds with others and engage in light-hearted interaction with those you find sexually appealing, the level of contentment you experience in your romantic relationships, your self-assurance and aptitude for tackling tasks with confidence, your open-mindedness in accepting feedback on your artistic endeavors, and your general sense of fulfillment across various aspects of your life.

What are the Consequences of the Sacral Chakra being Open and Blocked?

When the sacral chakra is in a state of openness and harmony, individuals experience an increased sense of sexual vitality and are capable of cultivating a fulfilling and contented partnership with their significant other. Furthermore, you exude a profound passion and enthusiasm for life as a whole, evoking sentiments of delight, happiness, and overall well-being. You demonstrate innovative thinking and possess a willingness to venture beyond conventional boundaries, displaying a readiness to embrace risks.

Furthermore, you possess the capacity to graciously embrace critique and harness it in a productive manner to enhance your personal growth.

Difficulties may arise in your emotional and romantic experiences once the sacral chakra becomes obstructed. Typically, this scenario begins with a sense of emotional volatility or lack of motivation, resulting in an internal disquietude regarding one's own self. It is also correlated with physiological and sexual impairment. Your libido diminishes and you encounter challenges in sustaining an affectionate connection with your partner. Furthermore, it is possible for individuals to encounter various forms of sexual compulsions.

Furthermore, an obstructed sacral chakra gives rise to symptoms such as decreased vitality, distress in the bladder, hypersensitivities, formations of kidney stones, dysfunctions in the urinary tract, hindered artistic expression, inability to conceive, infertility, and a significant decline in the experience of excitement and fervor. Additionally, you experience feelings of envy, distress, and dissatisfaction persistently, making it challenging for you to receive any form of critique, even when it is constructive and intended to be supportive in nature. In order to alleviate these issues, it is imperative to reinstate equilibrium within your sacral chakra.

What are the Techniques for Restoring Balance to the Sacral Chakra?

By diligently adhering to these measures consistently and over a duration of 3 to 4 weeks upon detecting symptoms of an imbalanced sacral chakra, you will effectively realign it.

Crystal Healing

Crystals and gemstones that possess an orange hue exhibit remarkable efficacy in restoring equilibrium to an obstructed sacral chakra. In order to alleviate energy obstructions within the sacral chakra, one may acquire Orange Calcite, Moonstone, Citrine, or Carnelian gemstones. One can choose to adorn oneself with any jewelry crafted from this material or alternatively, place it upon their nightstand and engage in a daily practice of holding it for a duration of 10 minutes to restore equilibrium to their sacral chakra.

Meditative Practice

Settle comfortably into your preferred posture within a tranquil environment free from any distractions or disturbances. Maintain proper posture by keeping your spine aligned, ensuring your limbs are in a relaxed state, and engaging in deep breathing exercises as previously instructed. Direct your focus towards the locus of the sacral chakra wherein lies your energy, and envision a circular shape tinted in orange, revolving gracefully at that very source. Imagine the intensifying expansion and illumination of the vibrant orange radiance as time elapses. Considering that the second chakra is associated with the element of water, envision the gentle radiance of orange extending in the likeness of serene undulating waves, gradually encompassing your entire being. Engage in this exercise for a duration of 10 to 20 minutes and should you repeat it twice a day, you will notice a gradual diminishment of all the difficulties linked to the sacral chakra.

Eat Right

Foods with an orange hue, such as papayas, oranges, peaches, mangoes, and yams, possess the ability to effectively restore equilibrium to one's sacral chakra. Furthermore, foods abundant in nutritious oils and beneficial fats, such as coconut and various seeds like poppy, sunflower, hemp, and pumpkin, play a stabilizing role in regulating it, along with the incorporation of meat-based broth. Incorporate these foods into your dietary regimen consistently to maintain a harmonious energy flow in your sacral chakra.

Affirmations

Engage in the repeated recitation of each of the subsequent affirmations, as well as any corresponding affirmations, with a minimum frequency of twice per day, as a means to achieve equilibrium within your sacral chakra.

I possess a strong belief in my capabilities and have a high level of self-assurance.

I possess the ability to cultivate mutually beneficial and fulfilling relationships.

I am deeply enthusiastic and fervent about embracing all aspects of life.

I am experiencing a robust state of physical well-being.

I am confident in my ability to engage in a sexually fulfilling, consensual, and mutually enjoyable manner.

I hold an affirmative outlook and consistently embrace opportunities for constructive development and transformation.

Partake in Aquatic Pursuits: Additionally, allocate time to partake in activities revolving around water, thereby maintaining a connection with the water element. It is recommended to engage in a warm bath on a nightly basis or opt for a brief, invigorating cold shower whenever desired. Additionally, dedicating time to frequent swimming or indulging in the pool facilitates relaxation. Alternatively, one may choose to immerse their feet in either cold or hot water, depending on personal preference, to achieve a state of repose.

Consistent utilization of these methodologies will expeditiously alleviate all energetic hindrances in the sacral chakra. In order to experience optimal well-being and contentment, it is imperative to cultivate a resilient and positive self-image, which is intricately influenced by the balance and vitality of the solar plexus energy center. The subsequent section elaborates extensively on this matter.

Healing The Fourth Chakra

The fourth chakra, known as the Anahata or heart chakra, is situated precisely at the midpoint of the thoracic region, encompassing the vicinity in and slightly above the cardiac region. It is exemplified by mammals and the existence of humanity, entwined with our visceral core and the realm of our emotions. By this point, it should have become apparent that the lower chakras are intricately connected to the individual in various ways, encompassing our most primal emotions and connections, progressing towards our sense of contentment, personal achievement, and self-assurance, and finally extending towards our interactions with others characterized by genuine fondness and empathy.

Our mesmeric chakra, the fourth in the series, exerts a profound impact on our interpersonal dynamics and our connections with the entities that coexist in this vast universe. It guides us in defining our approach to relationships, be it embracing them with euphoric bliss and open-mindedness or succumbing to somber anguish and trepidation. Consequently, it governs our relationship with the natural environment, the botanical realm, and our familial and societal ties. The heart chakra is the locus of the well-known 'Christ energy', which embodies our unwavering acceptance and profound joy in others. The sentiments linked with this chakra encompass compassion, affection, pardoning, understanding, reliance, our sense of emotional stability, and attaining a state of harmonious existence. If our heart chakra exhibits strength, we may experience a profound inclination towards philanthropic pursuits.

If there is an imbalance or misalignment in the heart chakra, it is possible for us to experience physical ailments such as respiratory or pulmonary issues, as well as gastrointestinal problems such as heartburn or other complications affecting the cardiovascular system. However, the primary manifestation of issues pertaining to this specific chakra is characterized by profound emotional distress, profound melancholy, and an overwhelming sense of internal hollowness. Any challenges related to matters of love, such as experiencing a lack of affection, questioning one's worthiness, or experiencing emotional instability, can be attributed to the activation or imbalance of this specific energy center in the body.

Associated fragrances: Lavender, yarrow, orris root, jasmine, meadowsweet, and marjoram

Herbs commonly found in association: Rue and saffron

Related glandular system: Thymus

Musical note: F

Phonetic representation of the Chakra sound: 'A' like in the words far, far, and car.

Element: Air

The following gemstones have been identified for their green hue: jade, aventurine, emerald, malachite, fluorite, ruby, moldavite, kunzite, rose quartz, chrysoprase, and pink tourmaline.

Color: Green or gold

Healing exercises:

Bikram yoga

Sufi heart practices (embrace and cultivate love)

Sun salutation (yoga)

GUIDELINES FOR ATTAINING EQUILIBRIUM IN THE SOLAR PLEXUS CHAKRA

Breathe deeply. Speak clearly. Compliment others. Spend time outdoors. Take a seat in the direct rays of the sun. Consider engaging in activities such as boxing, martial arts, Tai Chi, or belly dancing. Utilize a daily organizer or wall-mounted schedule. Document objectives and/or achievements. Plan a vacation. Finish a project. Register for an educational course. Engage in a conversation with a professional career or relationship counselor. Enhance proficiency in time management." "Develop effective time management techniques." "Optimize time management abilities." "Refine organizational skills pertaining to time management." "Strengthen time management competencies. Enroll in a program that focuses on enhancing assertiveness skills. Ensure you allocate sufficient time for contemplation before making a final decision. When requiring an increase in energy levels, it is advised to position your hand over the central part of your body. Grant yourself the privilege of utmost confidentiality and seclusion. Compose an individual mission statement. Examine the life and achievements of a influential figure by reviewing their biographical accounts or documentaries. Become a mentor. Perform community service. Embark on a spiritual journey of self-discovery. Please attempt the subsequent yoga asanas: upward-facing dog, downward-facing dog, and cat-cow.

THE HEART

Midst of the Thoracic Region – Verdant – Linkage

The heart chakra ought to be imbued with an abundance of affectionate energy. Gaining self-awareness through the exploration of the lower chakras ultimately cultivates a deep sense of empathy towards the entirety of the human race. These insightful emotions will awaken the soul and provide it with the necessary vitality to flourish. Compassion, peace, and stable relationships are good indicators of an abundant energy flow within the fourth chakra.

The absence of empathy has the potential to generate a formidable adverse current of energy. A disparity within the heart is defined by potent surges of resentment or anxiety. This energy will ultimately cultivate superfluous emotional barriers. Subsequently, a disposition characterized by insensitivity and criticism ensues. Additional manifestations linked to a disrupted heart chakra include tendencies towards codependence, expressions of aggression, withdrawal from social interactions, and a heightened focus on self-centeredness. Depression and addictions are indicative of a profound disparity in energy equilibrium.

Given that the fourth chakra is located within the thoracic region, it dispenses the necessary energy to maintain optimal well-being in that particular area of the body. This encompasses the cardiovascular system, including the cardiac muscle, vascular network, arterial pathways, pulmonary organs, mammary glands, thymus endocrine gland, and upper extremities. An energetic imbalance would be indicated by challenges pertaining to these anatomical regions. Asthma and allergies are frequently occurring medical conditions associated with the heart chakra. Another indication is discomfort experienced in the upper region of the back or shoulder areas. Serious attention should be given to significant imbalances that arise in relation to the heart, lungs, or breasts, as they can manifest as more extensive dysfunctions.

Methods for Achieving Equilibrium in the Cardiac Chakra

Spend time in nature. Consume fresh leafy greens and vegetables. Prepare an evening meal for an individual who holds a special place in your heart. Call a friend. Dispatch postcards. Embrace a cherished individual or clasp their palm. Read poetry. Watch a funny movie. Practice daily gratitude. Construct a visual composition featuring individuals held dearly in your heart. Seek self-discovery. Establish adequate physical and emotional boundaries. Establish a disciplined regimen focused on nurturing the spiritual self. Meditate. Engage in the practice of pranayama breathing exercises. Adopt a pet. Find your tribe. Receive therapeutic massage. Extend an apology when you have committed an offense against someone. Forgive others. Forgive yourself. Kindly attempt the subsequent yoga postures: downward-facing dog, cobra, and dancer pose.

THE THROAT

Respiratory Passage - Pale Cyan - Verbal Expression

An equilibrated throat chakra results in proficient communication abilities and the capacity to actively engage in listening, solely driven by the objective of comprehending. Lucid vocal projection, precise sense of timing, and overall cadence serve as indicators of a harmonious state of vitality. Furthermore, it is feasible to establish an inherent intuitive bond, thereby facilitating the audience of one's internal voice and the disclosure of personal endeavors and fervors.

Any disharmony in the energy dynamics of the throat chakra will constrict its natural flow, resulting in the stagnation rather than the unobstructed movement of energy. An individual experiencing an imbalance in this area may exhibit either excessive verbalization or complete reticence. Indications of an excessively unobstructed throat chakra manifest as deficient proficiency in communication, outbursts of intense emotions, incessant verbosity, or the expression of negative discourse. In contrast, an individual afflicted with a blocked chakra tends to exhibit reticence in their communication, concealing their genuine emotions. Furthermore, these detrimental energies inhibit the progression of individual endeavors and hinder the manifestation of creative ideas.

The fifth chakra governs the regions encompassing the throat, neck, and jaw. The dental region, gingival tissues, thyroid glands, and auditory organs are also intricately linked to this chakra. An impairment in any of these domains may indicate an inequilibrium. Mild to moderate surges in energy may manifest as a sore throat, toothache, or gum disease, whereas persistent earaches, neck pain, thyroid issues, or general illnesses could signal a more significant depletion of energy.

Chakra And Relationships

As it is commonly recognized, chakras are energetic focal points located within our spiritual essence. Every aspect of human existence falls under the domain of these entities, and as per the sacred Vedas, the sphere of romantic relationships is no exception. In the course of our existence, we shall encounter seven distinct categories of relationships, wherein each category will foster a unique state of mutual coherence between the individuals involved, closely aligned with the functioning of our seven chakras. According to the teachings of the Vedas, the primary chakra that exhibits the highest level of activity in your relationship will dictate your aspirations and objectives within the context of your partnership.

For instance, in the event that the predominant chakra in your relationship happens to be the root chakra, it will exert an influence on your beliefs and comprehension of contentment within your marital union, as it governs the forces associated with this aspect. The likelihood of experiencing discontentment is greater in the lower chakras—the root chakra and the solar plexus chakra—while the higher chakras—the heart, throat, third eye, and crown chakra—present greater potential for happiness. Nevertheless, there is no cause for dismay! It is imperative to bear in mind that one can progress through the various energy centers and allow the superior chakras to govern interpersonal connections. Let us now proceed to examine each relationship type in greater depth.

The couple associated with the root chakra will experience a significant influence from sexual energy due to the inherent connection of the root chakra with our fundamental instinctual drives. The driving force behind our desire to procreate and carry on our family lineage lies in the inherent sexual energy that compels us to ensure our survival by means of our offspring. The root chakra is additionally associated with the ego and self-centeredness, both of which hold significant relevance for individuals seeking to ensure their survival. Self-interest safeguards our necessities, while our self-image safeguards our sentiments.

The primary objective of the couple influenced by the root chakra is to engage in intimate experiences exclusively with one another. Typically, they convene at venues dedicated to social enjoyment, such as soirées, night establishments, and taverns. Please consider that couples who are imbued with higher chakras may also encounter each other in alternate settings, yet a distinction exists. The individuals guided by their higher chakras frequently happen upon such places when seeking a committed partnership.

The root chakra union is under the influence of the celestial body Mars, and upon embarking on their relationship, they experience a period characterized by profound intensity, akin to a honeymoon phase. Nevertheless, over time, the initial emotions will wane, leaving them with a sense of disillusionment and resentment. This initial phase of the relationship may give them the impression of being in love, but there will be an absence of requisite equilibrium within the partnership. The nature of the relationship will exhibit significant fluctuations, characterized by remarkable peaks and profound troughs. Their desire is solely to coexist, however, their feelings towards each other are void of affection, but rather rooted in emotional interdependence.

The subsequent form of relationship is characterized by the sacral chakra couple, in which the energy center associated with confidence, resourcefulness, and happiness is intricately connected to their bond. Nevertheless, it is also encompassed by their adverse characteristics of self-preservation, apprehension, and avarice. A pair that establishes a bond through their sacral chakra will cultivate a love that is rooted in their shared aspiration for affluence and convenience. The sacral chakra is subject to the influences exerted by the celestial body known as Venus. Upon their initial encounter, this couple shall discover serenity resonating at the sacral chakra level. With the passage of time, the potential for the root chakra to be unveiled shall also arise. As a consequence, both the difficulties and joys connected with the pairing of the root chakra will arise.

Nevertheless, the longings for contentment and affluence exhibited by the sacral chakra duo will establish a more steadfast basis for their partnership, in contrast to the requirements of the root chakra pair. Nonetheless, the sacral chakra is continue to be regarded as one of the more subordinate chakras, enduring fewer prospects for happiness in comparison to the chakras positioned higher in the spiritual hierarchy. Although there is no inherent wrongdoing in desiring a life of comfort, it is important to note that complications may arise when the pursuit of material prosperity becomes the primary objective within a relationship. This tendency is often observed in couples who are driven by the sacral chakra. This occurs as the individuals associated with the sacral chakra strive to attain a life of contentment and material abundance, desiring to possess a welcoming residence adorned with exquisite furnishings, luxurious automobiles, and similar amenities. It is imperative that they achieve financial prosperity jointly, with the potential for romantic love being an additional fortuitous outcome.

The solar plexus chakra is intricately linked to an array of aspirations and objectives, encompassing both refined and weighty endeavors. The opulent material indulgences encompass exquisite automobiles, possessions, residences, and so forth. These are the delights that the solar plexus couple requires. Moving beyond these mundane joys, it becomes apparent that individuals seek more refined versions of earthly material happiness, including influence, recognition, and distinction. It is unsurprising that numerous prominent individuals establish connections rooted in their solar plexus center. This energy centre is subject to the influence of the sun and motivates individuals to identify their role within the societal framework.

The couple associated with the solar plexus chakra possesses lofty aspirations for their future, necessitating concerted joint efforts to surmount these ambitions. It is imperative that they acquire the essential qualities of altruism and humility to transform their personal dispositions and genuinely cultivate a harmonious state of happiness in their relationship. Failing to accomplish this would perpetually deprive them of the opportunity to lead a contented life and transform their very essence. Initially, upon their initial encounter, they may engage in matrimonial union and diligently collaborate towards attaining the esteemed recognition and authority that they fervently desire. Once they successfully attain their objectives, contentious discussions will arise concerning their private affairs.

For instance, an individual may experience a deepening sense of pride in the achieved results, whereas the other individual may perceive their contribution as indispensable for the accomplishment to have taken place. These emotions have the potential to develop into deep-seated animosity. The objective of the solar plexus pair is to attain societal respect, achieve renown, wield authority, and garner prestige. The most optimal course of action for such a couple would be to refrain from intruding upon one another's lives.

Nevertheless, this becomes unattainable as they are in search of an individual to assist them in attaining their objectives.

The pairing of the heart chakra is positioned at the forefront among the elevated tiers of energy centers, rendering it precisely the initial one to exhibit escalated prospects for experiencing joy. They are typically the individuals who tend to have marriages that endure over time. They provide one another with the opportunity to resolve their karmic debts, purify their conscience, and actualize their life's purpose. Both individuals exhibit a profound level of enthusiasm and dedication as they diligently engage in the process of shaping their personalities and nurturing their personal growth. They possess a sincere desire for the happiness and well-being of those in their surroundings, and are highly likely to actively engage in philanthropy, volunteer work, and contribute to the betterment of their community. Should they acquire wealth without actively seeking it, they will employ it for the betterment of society as a whole.

The heart chakra couple faces few obstacles as they possess a deep understanding of one another and abide by the principle of seeking to bring happiness rather than suffering to their partner. Consequently, they refrain from causing harm to one another. They possess a robust and steadfast marital relationship, in addition to a substantial social circle. Nevertheless, they may encounter challenges; nevertheless, they will overcome them by fortifying their bond and intensifying their affection.

The duo of the laryngeal spiritual center, governed by the celestial body Mercury, aspires to align their perceptive faculties with the transcendental realm. In pursuit of this, they engage in the discipline of meditation, enabling them to perceive, sense, and comprehend the profound messages emanating from the cosmos. They aspire to bestow joy upon all individuals they encounter and contemplate. The cultivation of honesty and self-discipline is indispensable for the harmonious development of the throat chakra pair. They exercise restraint over their egocentric earthly emotions and refrain from succumbing to impulsivity driven by emotions. They possess a deep-seated bond and comprehensive grasp of the veracity. They decline to engage in conversations devoid of purpose and exhibit great modesty. It is widely believed that the consolidation of the throat chakra pairing facilitates the emergence of exceptionally gifted offspring who closely emulate the achievements of their progenitors.

Individuals who unite through the manifestation of the third eye chakra are subject to the celestial governance of the planet Saturn. They are the individuals who have diligently pursued self-realization throughout multiple lifetimes. Their objective as a collective is to engage in the pursuit of self-actualization in unison. Their exceptional synchronization on a psychic level is truly remarkable, enabling them to devote their entire existence to one another. Furthermore, they are obligated to pursue a deep understanding of the ultimate realities of the cosmos, as their ultimate goal is to attain a spiritual connection with the divine. This is an exceptionally uncommon bond, primarily attained by esteemed spiritual mentors. They prioritize the well-being and happiness of others above their own, exemplifying a couple who harbors genuine intentions to bring joy to others. They have made the decision to cohabit and adhere to one another as they embark upon a shared spiritual journey.

The final category of relationship encompasses the crown chakra couple, which is influenced by the celestial body known as Jupiter. This pair has the capacity to forge a love that is enchanting and ethereal. They refrain entirely from engaging in sexual activities. One partner regards the other as her mentor and guide, placing complete trust in their wisdom and knowledge. Faithfulness is imperative and enduring, never waning. They both exhibit the demeanor of a saint. Upon their demise from the terrestrial realm, they transcend to the ethereal domain, where an eternal coexistence can be observed. This represents their objective, and they will successfully achieve it. This form of love exhibits a significant level of elevation, much like the positioning of the crown chakra.

Every relationship category, as delineated in the Vedas, exhibits its own advantages and disadvantages. Should you find yourself in a chakra relationship type that does not align with your preferences, take solace in the certainty that you can transition towards the chakra relationship type of your choosing, just as we undertake the healing of each of our chakras.

Ensuring Equilibrium In Your Day-To-Day Existence

Upon embarking on the journey of awakening our chakras, it is paramount to uphold an elevated vibrational state, characterized by positive energy, throughout our everyday existence. Why? Due to the necessity of maintaining clear and protected energy and space, as well as sustaining a higher vibrational frequency, it is imperative to engage in the process of self-healing across multiple dimensions and the purification of our chakras from denser energies. This contributes to the preservation of chakra equilibrium.

1. Consistently foster mindfulness and engage in the practice of gratitude.

By consistently fostering a state of mindfulness, we are able to maintain a heightened sense of present awareness.

When we engage in deep contemplation and experience a sense of melancholy, we frequently fixate on previous events. When individuals encounter feelings of anxiety, they are engaging in a state of apprehension regarding forthcoming events or circumstances. Remaining in the current moment enables us to wholeheartedly be present for our own selves. Cultivating gratitude also enhances one's level of energy.

2. Sustain your energy levels through physical activity.

Maintaining regular clarity of mind, body, and spirit is of significant importance, whether through engaging in activities such as yoga, qigong, or other forms of physical exercise.

3. Indulge in the use of consecrated white sage.

The herb renowned as sacred white sage has been traditionally employed by Native Americans due to its potent capacity for purification. It effectively eliminates any detrimental energy from one's physical being or surrounding environment. Performing a purification ritual known as smudging involves the use of sacred white sage to cleanse a living space or oneself. To purify a residential setting, ignite the end of a cluster of sage with a match or lighter, permitting the smoke to billow. Employ your hand or a feather wand to gently disperse the smoke throughout the premises, commencing in a clockwise direction from the entrance, imbuing all objects with blessings as you advance. Repeat this ritual until you return to the front door. To conduct a smudging ritual on oneself, employ manual gestures to guide the ethereal smoke towards one's physical form, bestowing blessings upon each and every aspect of the body, with particular emphasis on the various energy centers aligning the central axis. While engaging in this activity, articulate, "I bestow blessings upon my arms, I bestow blessings upon my throat chakra, I bestow blessings upon my chest," and continue to do so for subsequent areas of focus. Ensure that you periodically dispose of the loose ashes into a receptacle that can withstand high temperatures as you progress.

4. Epsom salt baths.

It is advisable for women who possess a high sensitivity to the energy of others, to contemplate incorporating a practice of partaking in Epsom salt baths on a weekly or bi-weekly basis. This is equally applicable for individuals experiencing bodily discomfort, particularly those of a muscular nature.

Epsom salt comprises magnesium, which can be readily absorbed transdermally during bathing, thereby aiding in the alleviation of muscular and other bodily discomfort, while also aiding in stress management. Furthermore, it assists in purging auras, which proves particularly advantageous for individuals inclined to bring work to their residences, experience challenging commutes, work in environments with poisonous atmospheres, or regularly encounter formidable female colleagues. Epsom salt baths possess significant detoxifying properties for the body and can effectively serve as a preventive measure against common colds.

In the subsequent segment, we shall delve into an array of physical, emotional, mental, and spiritual maladies, manifestations, and encounters that manifest within our physical being when our chakras encounter disharmony. Furthermore, a comprehensive examination of the curative methodologies specifically targeting each sacral chakra will be undertaken.

Adrenal Fatigue

Adrenal fatigue is a condition that arises due to the prolonged exposure to persistent stress. The constant activation of the stress response places excessive demands on our adrenal glands, leading to inadequate adrenal functioning. In regular situations, the adrenal glands induce the secretion of cortisol, also referred to as the stress hormone, which assists us in managing stress. Adrenaline, which is known as the fight-or-flight hormone, is also activated by the adrenal glands. Both of these hormones are stimulated in order to facilitate our escape from tense circumstances. This is highly effective when employed in the context of short-term utilization. Nevertheless, individuals experiencing adrenal fatigue have been enduring prolonged periods of depletion due to persistent stress triggers.

Certain indicators of adrenal fatigue encompass overall fatigue, bodily discomfort, inexplicable reduction in body weight, decreased vascular pressure, dizziness, hair loss, and alterations in skin pigmentation (hyperpigmentation). Since the adrenals serve as the glands associated with both the root chakra and the sacral plexus chakra, it is important to investigate any concerns related to adrenal fatigue alongside efforts to identify and address the underlying sources of stress. Due to the fact that the root chakra pertains to matters concerning a sense of security, stability, and being grounded, it would be beneficial to examine any areas of imbalance within our lives. It is also pertinent to investigate matters pertaining to authority and self-worth, which are characteristics associated with the sacral plexus chakra.

Anxiety

Intermittent feelings of anxiety frequently manifest as a facet of one's routine daily existence. Nevertheless, if an overwhelming sense of unwavering apprehension engulfs our daily lives, it can have incapacitating consequences. For individuals afflicted with anxiety, it is plausible for their condition to escalate rapidly, giving rise to intense dread or panic within a condensed timeframe, ultimately triggering a panic attack. Frequently, it has the potential to disrupt our overall well-being.

Various types of anxiety can potentially implicate any of the chakras, depending on the specific nature of the condition. If our sacral plexus chakra becomes engaged, feelings of guilt or shame may drive our anxiety, typically relating to unresolved intense emotions. This phenomenon also occurs in instances when individuals experience anxiety stemming from previous traumas, particularly those related to sexual experiences. In the event that we experience a sense of unease or apprehension regarding our physical well-being in the contemporary society pertaining to fundamental aspects such as sustenance, accommodation, financial stability, among others, it indicates that our fundamental energy center known as the root chakra is in a state of imbalance, thereby consistently engendering within us a feeling of persistent survival instinct.

Back Pain

Discomfort experienced in any region of the back, whether it be the upper, middle, or lower back, without the influence of physical trauma or repetitive physical strain, could potentially indicate a correlation with the well-being of the chakras. Pain can vary in intensity, ranging from a persistent, dull sensation that causes tension in the back, to a sudden, sharp pain that restricts the ability to move freely.

LOWER BACK

When individuals encounter difficulties in their material prosperity, interpersonal connections, artistic manifestations; repressing emotions or failing to adequately address them; facing challenges related to survival and attaining fundamental provisions, they might experience discomfort and strain in the lumbar region. We might experience heightened discomfort in the back region, particularly in instances unrelated to physical injury, when we perceive a lack of financial support.

Codependency

Codependency is a term used to describe the state of being in a dysfunctional, imbalanced relationship, characterized by an excessive reliance on our partner to fulfill our emotional and psychological needs. Codependency can also be characterized by a relationship wherein one partner consistently facilitates the irresponsible behavior or addiction of another individual, with the former frequently disregarding their own needs and desires in order to assist the latter. This can extend to a degree where the sacrificing partner relinquishes aspects of their own identity, exhibits inadequate boundaries and diminished self-worth, experiences insecurity, and struggles to effectively express distressing emotions. Due to the fact that codependent relationships typically arise from apprehensions surrounding abandonment and rejection, a direct correlation can be observed between these relationships and the primary chakra, where actions and emotions grounded in fear originate.

Codependency frequently emerges during early stages of development, as a result of a dysfunctional family system that disregards or invalidates experiences of emotional distress, apprehension, indignation, or humiliation. This may encompass scenarios where a family member is grappling with addiction, occasions involving instances of physical, emotional, or sexual abuse, or situations wherein a family member is enduring a persistent mental or physical ailment. The root chakra is also connected to matters arising from unaddressed family distress.

In situations of codependency, an inequity can also arise within the heart chakra, predominantly stemming from our directed attention towards affection for others rather than fostering self-love, a facet that is frequently neglected. It entails a disconnection from the core of our emotional being. When there is an imbalance in this particular chakra, it may result in a diminished capacity for discernment in interpersonal connections.

Due to the challenges posed to our self-esteem when engaged in a codependent relationship, it has been observed that our solar plexus chakra is similarly impacted. If the equilibrium of our sacral plexus chakra is disrupted, emotions related to shame, guilt, anger, and resentment will manifest within a codependent relationship, along with an absence of properly established boundaries.

Guilt

Guilt is the emotional response arising from the belief or acknowledgement of having engaged in a wrongful act, irrespective of the veracity of the perception. This sentiment is frequently associated with the sacral plexus chakra, which serves as the locus of our emotions. This particular energy center is also linked to the experience of pleasure and the sentiments associated with our sexuality. If individuals were conditioned to suppress their sexuality and/or emotions during their formative years, they frequently experience feelings of guilt and shame during their adult years. Guilt serves the purpose of ensuring our behavior remains in proper alignment. However, typically, this is an inefficient state of mind that impedes our ability to derive enjoyment, and the optimal experience of pleasure occurs when our sacral plexus chakra achieves equilibrium.

Hip Pain

When individuals encounter discomfort in the hip region, including tightness, tension, muscle spasms, or pain, without any connection to physical trauma or excessive physical exertion, it is frequently indicative of an association with imbalances in the sacral plexus chakra. Frequently, the hips tend to retain a substantial reservoir of suppressed emotions, typically those that have not been effectively addressed or consciously acknowledged, often as a result of deliberate avoidance.

Due to the fact that the sacral plexus chakra serves as the dwelling place for our emotions, an imbalance within this region is created when we fail to acknowledge and give due respect to our emotional responses in relation to a particular circumstance. Furthermore, if we are encountering difficulties in openly embracing a nourishing sense of sexuality, particularly with regards to the shame associated with our sexual identity (which can indicate an imbalance in the sacral plexus chakra), such experiences can also lead to tension or discomfort in the hip region.

Infertility

When a woman is unable to achieve conception despite continuous efforts for a minimum duration of one year, it is classified as infertility. While it is true that numerous individuals encounter challenges with fertility, the perplexity and apprehension that women endeavoring to conceive undergo give rise to considerable stress, occasionally leading to feelings of shame. The involvement is attributed to the sacral plexus chakra, owing to its association not only with the reproductive organs but also due to its function as the locus of our emotional experiences. A significant number of women facing infertility encounter intense emotional struggles, prompting them to question the validity of their decisions by pondering inquiries such as: "Is this the appropriate course of action?" "Do I truly desire parenthood?" "Am I partnered with the suitable individual?" "What if I lack the ability to adequately care for a child?" and "How will this transformation impact my life?"

Occasionally, the root of the issue can be attributed to physiological factors, including suboptimal egg quality, diminished sperm count, absence of menstruation, heightened levels of follicle-stimulating hormone (FSH), or other related complications. However, on numerous occasions, women who are attempting to conceive often experience heightened levels of stress. Due to the potential link between infertility and familial challenges, it can be inferred that the root chakra is also implicated. Additional factors related to the root chakra that may be of concern to women who are attempting to conceive emerge when they lack assistance from crucial family members or harbor apprehensions about transmitting undesirable familial attributes to their progeny. Additionally, due to the potential impact on an individual's self-esteem and the sense of loss of control over their physical being, solar plexus chakra complications may arise, as this energy center serves as our source of empowerment.

Sexual Abuse

When subjected to sexual violation, the resultant mistreatment can inflict profound harm, impacting not only our physical well-being but also our intrinsic essence. As a result of the traumatic experience, individuals who have encountered sexual abuse may exhibit emotional numbness or disconnection from their own selves as a coping mechanism to evade profound suffering. They might experience feelings of shame and potentially attribute responsibility to themselves for the incident (despite the fact that the traumatic event was not at all their fault). Changes in their sexual orientation and emotional responses to pleasure may occur. Furthermore, as the power dynamic was utilized in that particular instance, it is possible that control-related concerns may arise. The anger surrounding the incident, directed towards themselves, and/or their abuser, is frequently repressed. These responses are all comprehensible, considering the profound nature of the trauma, and are all connected to the sacral plexus chakra.

If the instance of sexual abuse was executed by a relative, and in the event that significant family members displayed a lack of support upon discovering the trauma, it is plausible for sentiments of betrayal to surface, which are intricately linked to the foundational chakra. Moreover, in the absence of proper processing, the persistent pain may exert an adverse influence on one's overarching self-assurance and self-respect, which bear a significant connection to the solar plexus chakra. The violation may also have a direct impact on the throat chakra, leading survivors to experience a sense of being silenced and inhibited in expressing themselves verbally (or at least feeling uneasy in doing so). The paradox lies in the fact that engaging in activities that stimulate the throat chakra, such as expressing oneself and recounting personal experiences, can have a therapeutic effect, benefiting not only the survivor but also those who can derive strength and inspiration from their narrative. Expressing your emotions to individuals with whom you have a sense of security may evoke a sense of apprehension, yet it has the potential to facilitate the progression towards personal and emotional restoration.

Sexually Transmitted Diseases (STDs)

In the event of persistent instances of sexually transmitted infections and diseases, it is possible that an obstruction or disharmony exists within the sacral plexus chakra. This chakra deals with our perceptions of our sexuality, particularly how we express it, and the emotional aspects (versus the physical aspects). Frequently, shame significantly contributes to the recurrence of sexually transmitted infections. There is a significant correlation between perceiving ourselves as engaging in promiscuous behavior and experiencing intense feelings of shame, which coincides with the reoccurrence of STIs.

This could serve as evidence that we ought to examine or scrutinize our perspectives regarding what we consider to be acceptable manifestations of sexual behavior. It may be valuable to evaluate the precision or relevance of our own sexual self-perceptions. Frequently, they are obsolete, and we persist in being influenced by lingering feelings of guilt or regret stemming from previous experiences. At times, individuals may also experience instances of physical, emotional, or sexual abuse, which can profoundly influence their perception of themselves in relation to their sexuality. When we manage to rectify our perspectives regarding our sexual identity in a constructive manner, we simultaneously restore the balance and well-being of our sacral plexus chakra.

Shame

Shame arises when we endure humiliation, stemming from either our perception of having committed a wrongdoing or from an event that implies our insufficiency, inadequacy, or lack of strength. Occasionally, there may be moments when we experience a sense of disgrace regarding our true identity, our conduct in public settings, instances of failure, and our innermost sentiments pertaining to our sexuality.

The multitude of intense emotions disrupts the harmony of the sacral plexus chakra, which serves as the center for our emotional state. Indeed, due to the fact that this focal point of energy is also the repository for emotions pertaining to sex and sexuality, individuals frequently encounter feelings of shame in relation to their physical forms. Due to the potential impact of shame on our personal empowerment and self-perception (often leading to a decrease in self-value as a means of self-retribution for perceived transgressions), the solar plexus chakra is also negatively affected, placing a burden on our self-confidence.

Benign uterine neoplasms and fluid-filled sacs in the uterus

As per the Mayo Clinic, uterine fibroids are benign proliferations of the uterus that commonly manifest during the reproductive phase of a woman's life. Numerous instances arise where women encounter uterine fibroids at some point in their lifetime. On certain occasions, they may not give rise to any symptoms. Nevertheless, on occasions, they have the potential to attain considerable dimensions and induce discomfort during menstruation, defecation, and digestion, ultimately impacting respiration. Cysts refer to fluid-filled sacs that are situated either inside, or within, the ovaries.

When an anomalous proliferation occurs within the uterine region, it frequently indicates an imbalance within the sacral plexus chakra. Due to the presence of physical obstructions in the reproductive region, the energy body is indicating the existence of impeded creative flow and energy. It is possible that you are harboring outdated, adverse, and detrimental thoughts, emotions, or feelings that are redirecting life energy towards unproductive endeavors. These could pertain to occupations or associations that you have surpassed in growth, or to disputes concerning innovation, prosperity, procreation, and/or personal connections within your life.

Sacral Chakra Meditations

The sacral chakra can alternatively be referred to as the Svadhisthana. This is a term derived from Sanskrit, where 'sea' represents the self and 'adhisthana' denotes establishment. This chakra, known as the second chakra, is associated with sentiments, artistic expression, and physical pleasure. The chakra in question is associated with the element of water, which consequently imparts to it an energy that is distinguished by a supple and unhindered movement. The sacral chakra is situated in close proximity to the abdominal region's central area, approximately three inches above the navel. Located in the posterior region, it can be observed at the lumbar vertebrae level. This chakra is also interconnected with the lymphatic system within the human body. The sacral chakra serves as the focal point for the range of feelings or emotions that one may encounter. It is directly associated with your sexuality. This particular energy center, known as the chakra, is driven by the pursuit of pleasure. By unlocking and activating this chakra, you will be able to vividly experience and connect with the sensations arising from your immediate surroundings.

Diagnosing an obstructed sacral chakra.

The sacral chakra is associated with one's emotional wellbeing and sexual energy. It will facilitate your comprehension of various phenomena across the world, such as the intrinsic dynamics of opposing forces.

When an obstruction occurs within this particular energy center, it will give rise to the inhibition of emotions, heightened susceptibility, feelings of guilt, and tendencies towards obsessive-compulsive behavior, among other manifestations. It will diminish your zest for life and render you susceptible to addictive behavior.

In the event of an underactive state of this chakra, the tendency to suppress one's emotions may arise. It is crucial for individuals to have the capacity to openly convey their emotions to others. This will hinder the expression of emotions.

In the event of an overactive state of this particular chakra, an excess of emotional manifestations shall manifest themselves more profusely than is deemed appropriate. There lacks equilibrium, potentially resulting in heightened sensitivity or emotional reactivity. It will engender a loss of self-control over impulses and foster a proclivity towards manipulation for personal advantage. Furthermore, it could potentially prompt you to partake in improper sexual behavior.

There exist numerous health concerns associated with a displaced or disrupted sacral chakra:

- Urinary and vesical ailments
- Impaired renal function
- Issues related to the colon
- Discomfort experienced in the lumbar region
- Issues of a sexual nature such as sexual dysfunction
- Issues pertaining to the pelvic region or hips
- You are also likely to encounter emotional challenges, such as struggles with forging commitments or facing complications in relationships.

Achieving equilibrium in your sacral chakra

On occasion, individuals may be encountered who exude genuine authenticity and a welcoming demeanor from the initial interaction. Despite their amiable nature, they will not appear excessively dependent or overly assertive in their interactions. This individual possesses a well-maintained sacral chakra. They exhibit a propensity for being receptive to the individuals in their vicinity. Nevertheless, there could be instances in which individuals of this nature also encounter an asymmetry within their sacral chakra. During such instances, there exist straightforward approaches through which equilibrium may be reinstated in the sacral chakra.

Yoga poses to facilitate hip opening

During yoga classes, it is commonly stated by instructors that individuals have a tendency to accumulate tension within their hip region. This situation has the potential to give rise to both emotional and physical tension. It exhibits a direct correlation with the sacral chakra. Should you have any reservations regarding this, I encourage you to engage in a practice of mindfulness by observing the contraction of your muscles in moments of heightened stress. It can be observed that this phenomenon typically occurs in the vicinity of the hips, lower abdomen, or throat. The hip joints exhibit the capacity for movement across numerous orientations. You may endeavor to practice yoga poses aimed at enhancing hip flexibility across a comprehensive spectrum of movements. An alternative approach would be to place your attention on maintaining a single pose and releasing any tension. The cow pose is an excellent choice for an introductory posture. An alternative can be to experiment with the posture of the bound angle.

Engage in unrestricted movements on the dance floor

Dance serves as a highly effective means of energizing and balancing the sacral chakra. If you desire solitude, simply shut your door, indulge in melodious tunes, and engage in a joyful dance to your fullest satisfaction. It would be more advantageous to partake in uninhibited dancing alongside companions.

Improve your physical fitness

Maintaining physical fitness will contribute to achieving a harmonious equilibrium in the sacral chakra. In order for your muscles to maintain their overall well-being, it is imperative that they possess sufficient strength. The practice of yoga asanas aids in restoring physical vitality and sculpting the body to its former state of tone. Additionally, it will promote the well-being of your mental and emotional state. Many individuals experience weight gain in their lower abdominal area, making it an ideal starting point for addressing this concern. Attempt various positions that specifically target the lower abdominal muscles, such as the boat pose or the pendant pose. Yogic leg lifts are advantageous as well.

Experiment with visualizations featuring the color orange" "Engage in the utilization of visual representations showcasing the hue of orange" "Explore the option of employing orange-themed visualizations" "Employ visual aids that incorporate the color orange

The hue associated with the sacral chakra is that of the color orange. Attempt to mentally imagine a radiant, luminous hue emanating from the area situated in the lowermost portion of your abdominal region. One can project this radiant aura to any desired area of their body using their breath.

Verify the equilibrium of the remaining chakras.

Should there be a disparity in a singular chakra, it shall have an impact on the equilibrium of the remaining chakras. Therefore, in the event of detecting an asymmetry in the sacral chakra, it is highly likely that there exists a corresponding imbalance in another chakra as well. The sacral chakra and the throat chakra are intricately linked. While engaging in the practice of hip opening poses, it is advisable to direct one's attention towards the throat region, and to take note of any sensations of release that may be experienced in that vicinity. Please consider attempting the fire log pose for this. Another beneficial posture to consider is the bridge pose, as it facilitates the synchronization of multiple chakras simultaneously. Take a deliberate pace while endeavoring to synchronize your motions with your respiration.

It is imperative that you release your grip.

It is possible that you are already familiar with this information, but it is imperative that you give it your undivided attention at this moment. It is imperative for one to acquire the ability to relinquish anything that is no longer beneficial or conducive to their personal growth and enrichment. One should release any adverse thoughts, memories, emotions, or individuals from their consciousness. Removing this burden will generate ample room in your life for more auspicious opportunities and a tide of constructive energy.

Upon achieving equilibrium in your sacral chakra, you will discover a heightened overall willingness to engage in emotional vulnerability with others. You will develop a heightened sense of intuition and build trust in others. Do not isolate yourself due to a handful of negative encounters. There will consistently be individuals of merit as well.

Indications of obstruction

In the event of an obstruction in the sacral chakra, one may encounter the subsequent indications:

- Establishing deep emotional or romantic bonds with others may prove challenging for you.

- You might encounter sensations of distress or bewilderment.

- You may develop a sense of apprehension towards others and may begin to question their affection towards you.

You are likely to encounter difficulties in cultivating a positive self-perception.

- It is possible that you may encounter numerous unfruitful and detrimental relationships.

- One might experience a negative perception or fear towards engaging in sexual activities.

Restoring balance to your sacral chakra. Revitalizing your sacral energy center.

Rejuvenating and harmonizing your sacral chakra. Promoting the healing of your sacral energy center. Cultivating a state of harmony and wellness in your sacral chakra.

Below, we present a selection of the most effective methods through which one may facilitate the healing of their sacral chakra:

Engage in the process of emotional purging

Purge out your emotions. Do not allow emotions to accumulate within you and adversely impact your well-being. Employ any methods at your disposal to alleviate the accumulation of said emotions. You have the freedom to openly express your emotions by shedding tears or engaging in exuberant physical expressions. The decision rests solely in your hands; simply seek out something that will provide assistance.

Demonstrate your creative expression "

There exist numerous artistic endeavors in which you can engage your talents. Attempt engaging in activities such as sketching, capturing images through photography, preparing culinary dishes, creating sculptures, or exploring any other subjects that spark your interest. Explore various artistic mediums through which you may channel your creative self-expression. It is within your reach to pursue a career in writing, should you desire to do so. There is no expectation to achieve mastery in any of these endeavors. Simply utilize them as a means to express your thoughts and emotions. It is possible that you will develop an affection for it.

Determine any impediments related to sexual function/growth

You may have been influenced by certain biases or societal norms regarding sexuality throughout the course of your life. Please contemplate these matters and compile a comprehensive inventory. Do you believe that these had an impact on you? If this is the case, you may consider obtaining assistance in order to address any sexual obstacles you may be experiencing. Illuminating any detrimental assumptions that may impede your progress in the future is of utmost significance.

Utilize the practice of crystal healing to alleviate any obstructions within the sacral chakra

There is an abundance of crystals such as jasper, moonstone, and carnelian that can be employed for the purpose of healing the sacral chakra. Utilize them as adornments or incorporate them into mindfulness exercises. They will aid in enhancing the harmonious circulation of energy within this chakra.

Exercise caution in regard to emotional stimuli.

Take heed of the factors that elicit unfavorable emotions or responses within your being. When experiencing feelings of anger or distress, it is advisable to pause momentarily, collect oneself, and engage in deep breathing exercises. Exercise mindfulness regarding your emotions, yet refrain from allowing them to dominate your thoughts and actions.

Practice self-care

Do not allow yourself to entertain negative thoughts regarding your physical appearance. Embrace yourself as you are. The body size or skin color of an individual holds no significance. You possess inherent uniqueness as an individual, and it is imperative to embrace oneself in its entirety. Please refrain from apologizing for your weight, regardless of whether you perceive it as excessive or insufficient. If individuals are grappling with body image concerns or eating disorders, it is advised that they seek out support groups as a means of facilitating their path towards healing. Many individuals face challenges of this nature, and engaging in these communities can facilitate personal growth and foster self-acceptance. If you aspire to improve your overall well-being, you can proactively embrace a nutritious diet and engage in regular physical activities. However, it is important to emphasize that this pertains solely to your individual welfare, rather than conforming to societal norms dictating appearance.

Investigate the underlying factors contributing to any addiction you may be experiencing.

Individuals resort to coping mechanisms such as addiction as a means of escaping their everyday circumstances or challenges. Engage in self-inquiry to ascertain the underlying cause of your addiction and address it accordingly. At what point in time did you initially develop this dependency? What made you start? Was someone responsible for influencing your decision? Gaining insight into the root cause will assist you in successfully managing and ultimately conquering your addiction over an extended duration. If you are grappling with a severe addiction, it is imperative that you seek professional assistance. Regardless of the duration of your addiction, you are capable of achieving recovery by fostering a determined mindset. The task ahead might pose challenges, but the rewards will be commensurate with your dedication. Eliminating detrimental dependencies will aid in the restoration and harmonization of your sacral chakra.

Upon the complete healing and subsequent opening of your sacral chakra, you shall observe the manifestations outlined below:

- You will develop a heightened sense of self-acceptance and acknowledge the influential nature of your sexuality.

- You will engage in mutually satisfying intimate relationships with individuals who treat you well, promoting physical and emotional well-being.

You will cultivate a more robust sense of self-worth and command admiration from others too.

Adornments of precious metals and gemstones, as well as natural crystals aligned with the body's energy centers.

The subsequent stones and gemstones are suitable for the purpose of healing the sacral chakra:

- The gemstone referred to as citrine
- The mineral known as vanadinite
- The gemstone known as carnelian

- Blue-green aquamarine • Cyan-blue turquoise • Teal-colored turquoise • Azure-hued turquoise

- Fluorite of a blue-green hue.

- Calcite in the color orange

Yoga and meditation practices tailored to balance the sacral chakra.

The subsequent yoga methodologies are efficacious for the purpose of attaining balance and activating the sacral chakra:

The asana known as Malasana, or commonly referred to as Squat Pose, ...

In this posture, it is necessary to internally rotate the hips, while simultaneously elevating the sternum towards the celestial zenith. You are advised to maintain this posture for approximately ten breaths, as doing so contributes to the development of strength and flexibility in the feet, ankles, and hips. When assuming a squatting position, it is advisable to activate the pelvic floor muscles in a manner that facilitates a poised and robust suspension. A dynamic succession is formed upon transitioning into the Uttanasana or erect forward fold posture. Subsequently, assume the squat position once more following the Uttanasana.

Baddha Konasana, commonly known as Bound Angle Pose,...

You will have the opportunity to perform extensive stretches targeting the muscles of the inner thighs and groin. Furthermore, one can facilitate a smooth transition into this posture. Attempt to perform a continuous, rhythmic vertical movement of the knees, resembling the motion of fluttering. Maintain this stance with the knees in an extended position, and proceed to gradually lower the upper body by directing the chest and head towards the feet during the process of bending forward. To achieve an upward position once more, you should vertically ascend by sequentially flexing each segment of the spinal column. You may perform this action multiple times.

The gesture known as Ushas Mudra, also referred to as the Mudra of Breaking Dawn

This mudra can be performed while in a seated posture. Ensure that your hands are placed calmly and comfortably on your lap. One must intertwine the digits of both hands whilst applying pressure to the right thumb with the left thumb positioned atop it. This action will complete the mudra gesture, and it is recommended that you maintain this posture for approximately 10 to 15 minutes on a daily basis. The optimal time to engage in this activity would be during the early hours of the morning, subsequent to awakening from sleep. It will promote hormonal balance and facilitate the cultivation of a positive emotional state for the day ahead. It will enhance your cognitive acuity and is a mudra that promotes a sense of well-being.

The asana known as Ustrasana, or commonly referred to as the camel pose,

The camel pose presents an excellent opportunity to effectively stretch the muscles in the hip flexors. Furthermore, it will aid in facilitating the transfer of energy from the Earth into your physical being. It is recommended that you actively involve your core muscles to aid in safeguarding your spinal column. Engage your core by drawing your navel towards the spine and simultaneously extend the tailbone downwards towards the ground as you attempt a backbend. In the course of this exercise, should you experience a pronounced sensation of compression in the lower lumbar area, it is advisable to provide support to the lower back by utilizing your hands, as opposed to attempting to reach for your feet. Should you experience any sensation of pressure in the neck area, it is advisable to draw your chin inward towards your chest rather than extending the throat upwards towards the sky. This posture is to be maintained for a duration of five to ten breaths. One should ensure that each inhalation is unhurried and substantial. Upon transitioning from the posture, employ your hands to provide assistance to the lumbar region as you gradually descend your hips towards the heels. Please maintain this position briefly prior to proceeding.

The mantra of Svadhisthana chakra is also known as the Bija mantra VAM.

Yoga transcends mere physical postures, encompassing the harmonization of sounds and vibrations as well. The auditory and tactile stimuli associated with the sacral chakra can be expressed through the phonetic representation of 'VAM'. Enunciation of this sound will result in the pronunciation closest to 'V-

UH-M'. During the act of chanting, it is imperative to direct your focus towards the lower pelvis, as this will yield the most substantial effect. If you find yourself in a public setting, it is also feasible to recite the mantra internally.

Engaging in a Chakra meditation focused on Svadhisthana, also known as the sacral chakra

The Svadhisthana chakra is the second chakra, located approximately three to four centimeters above the genital area. This particular chakra assumes the responsibility of governing the flow of sexual energy and fostering creativity. Several postures aid in the stimulation of Svadhisthana Chakra, and Sukhasana is deemed particularly appropriate for this purpose. To execute Sukhasana, one must assume a seated position, with eyes gently shut and the spine maintained in an upright posture. You must direct your complete attention and endeavor to maintain utmost stillness throughout the duration of the posture. Additionally, it is worth considering that selecting suitable music that aligns with your emotional state would undeniably enhance the effectiveness of your meditation practice. Following that, direct your concentration towards the meditation practice for a duration of 30 minutes, wherein you will observe the awakening of this particular chakra, accompanied by a profound sense of bliss and equilibrium.

Dietary considerations

To restore balance to the sacral chakra, it is advisable to incorporate a greater quantity of sweet fruits and nuts into your diet. Consume a higher quantity of coconuts, passion fruits, melons, mangoes, and strawberries. Nourish the chakra with energy-infused foods such as honey, almonds, or walnuts. Spices recommended for this particular chakra encompass caraway seeds, sesame seeds, vanilla, and sweet paprika.

Additionally, incorporate foods that are abundant in omega-three fatty acids such as salmon into your dietary intake. These factors will aid in the reduction of bodily inflammation and enhancement of cardiovascular well-being. It is imperative that you maintain proper hydration as water functions as the fundamental element associated with the sacral chakra. It encompasses a range of beverages, including plain water, herbal teas, and coconut water.

Positive declarations for the sacral chakra

Achieving Equilibrium in Your Sacral Chakra.

Assume a relaxed posture, keeping your arms and legs in an uncrossed position.

Inhale deeply through the nostrils and exhale through the mouth for a series of three repetitions.

Place your hand on your umbilicus. Perform a rotational motion in a clockwise direction and verbally utter the following words:

I acknowledge and embrace my emotions, allowing them to flow through me effortlessly.

My emotions are balanced.

I experience an overpowering sense of inner tranquility.

I am liberated from the necessity of resorting to any self-soothing substances or behaviors that dampen my emotions.

I epitomize radiance, beauty, and strength while embracing a vibrant and enriching existence.

I possess a remarkable aptitude for creativity and currently offer a significant and valuable contribution to the world we inhabit.

I am cultivating a positive self-care routine through the use of affirming language and emotions.

Perform the actions and recite the statements a total of four to five instances.

Gently shut your eyes and inhale deeply, allowing the warm glow of the orange light to permeate your being, directing its energy towards your sacral chakra. Experience the gradual expansion of this light within you, as it brings forth a heightened sense of illumination and vitality.

Please articulate the following phrase with vocalization: "I affirm that my Sacral chakra is currently harmonized and infused with renewed vitality." Therefore, it is so."

Engaging In A Meditative Practice For The Sacral Chakra: "Invocation Of Vom"

The Sacral chakra governs an individual's artistic expression and emotional essence. When confronted with such issues, individuals may encounter challenges in managing their emotions and engaging in social interactions. Furthermore, it can also result in diminished self-esteem and self-value, and may even give rise to challenges pertaining to one's own sexual identity. To achieve equilibrium in the sacral chakra through meditation, it is recommended to assume the Vajra Asana posture in yoga, characterized by sitting on the knees. This role offers advantages for the lower extremities and potentially supports the process of digestion. Once comfortably positioned in the Vajra Asana posture, it is customary to extend the hands with the palms facing upwards. It is recommended to keep the hands positioned at the lower abdomen in close proximity to the navel. The left hand should provide support for the right hand, as it will serve as the guiding force for the energy. After you have prepared yourself, commence the process of mental imagery by visualizing the chakra, ideally perceiving it as a spherical manifestation of vibrant orange energy. During this activity, it is advised to engage in nasal breathing exclusively as a means to promote relaxation. The sacral chakra pertains to the element of water; therefore, employing calcite or tiger's eye crystals may be beneficial in the process of restoring its balance. The sacral mantra is articulated as "Vowm" in pronunciation.

Opening Your Chakras

The act of harmonizing and activating the chakras facilitates the revival of the equilibrium and vitality within the energetic framework. When one's chakras are open and harmonized, a sense of clarity, overall well-being, tranquility, and complete embodiment is experienced. Life is perceived as being within one's capacity to handle with a sense of contentment, rather than being inundated or burdened with stress. Every action is infused with a profound tranquility when one's chakras are harmonized and receptive.

What does the process of achieving Chakra equilibrium entail?

When the concept of chakra balancing is brought up, it typically encompasses a range of interpretations and methodologies. A commonly accepted interpretation of this concept refers to achieving a state of equilibrium among the chakras. The notion of chakra opening and balancing solely considers a fraction of the entirety, as each individual chakra constitutes merely a component of the overarching system. Upon gaining an understanding of the functioning of these energy systems, it becomes apparent that they possess a significant interconnection and engage in perpetual interaction within the realm of our existence. This implies that the process of opening and harmonizing one's chakras involves considering the interconnectedness of each component in conjunction with the entire system.

What are the methods and reasons behind this process?

Methodology: Within the context of this literary composition, we shall embark upon an investigation into a variety of methodologies aimed at the mending and expansion of the chakra system. These methodologies encompass the utilization of gemstone therapy, Reiki energy manipulation, and the implementation of affirmations during chakra meditation exercises.

Why? The purpose of harmonizing the chakras is to restore equilibrium to the energetic channels that facilitate vital life force. In ordinary existence, a multitude of endeavors unfailingly transpire, necessitating our focus, inducing stress, and influencing our levels of vitality. Some activities can be exhausting, whereas others can be enriching and deeply satisfying. Furthermore, past experiences and occurrences hold the capacity to exert a protracted impact on our emotional state, as well as our sense of belonging and vitality in this world.

Our daily lives are characterized by numerous obligations and responsibilities, resulting in persistent stress that impedes the proper alignment of our chakras and disrupts the natural flow of our personal energy. This phenomenon impacts the quantity of energy circulating within the energy systems, subsequently obstructing the flow of energy through our chakras and resulting in the formation of blockages. As a result of this phenomenon, certain chakras may become hyperactive in order to restore balance, leading to an excessive amount of energy.

Chakra Healing for the Optimization of our Energetic Matrix: "

Addressing the chakras involves the restoration of an unwavering and effective circulation of energy in areas where it is deficient, rectifying any excessive energy levels, and ultimately reinstating bodily equilibrium. The process of healing these energy systems involves exerting influence over and regulating the flow of energy, while ensuring that it is adjusted to attain its optimal capacity and motion. An ideally functioning chakra system will possess the subsequent attributes:

Equilibrium and Balance Overall.

Achieving Optimal Intensity in the Chakras.

Accurate Alignment of the Chakra Rotation.

The Accurate Direction, Both Outward and Inward.

It is important to observe that chakras operate interdependently, employing a intricate and fluid network of focal points that function harmoniously as a cohesive entity. Comprehending the precise significance of chakra healing necessitates a deep awareness of the distinct functions associated with each chakra, as well as their interconnectedness within the holistic chakra system. There are numerous modalities available for the restoration and channeling of healing energies, encompassing both ancient customs and age-old knowledge. A widely practiced technique for initiating and harmonizing one's chakras involves engaging in the practice of meditation.

Utilizing Meditation Techniques to Align and Restore the Chakras:

Numerous beneficial chakra meditations center on the ramifications and origins of bodily imbalances, encompassing the resultant emotions and cognitive conditions. One should begin by introspecting and determining the root cause of their suffering and distress.

What factors contribute to the experience of stress in our daily lives? Human suffering arises from the belief of our detachment from the universe, rather than recognizing our inherent connection to the entirety of existence. This can be likened to an oceanic ripple, diligently seeking water, oblivious to the fact that it is already comprised of water itself. Our notions regarding our inherent essence as humans give rise to our anguish, manifesting when we perceive ourselves as detached from the interconnectedness of all existence. This statement renders us perpetually unsatisfied, regardless of our life circumstances.

What is the mechanism by which meditation resolves this issue? When we are capable of perceiving ourselves as the consciousness that exists beyond reality, encompassing all existence, our thoughts and emotions have the potential to reveal genuine tranquility. We possess a inherent understanding that we are interconnected with all things, yet our cognitive faculties impede this knowledge and persuade us to believe otherwise. Meditation serves as a means to regain a profound connection with this innate truth.

In the practice of chakra meditation, we are affording our chakras the requisite room for achieving harmony and self-restoration. The meditations that prove to be most effective for this purpose focus on the realignment of our consciousness with true awareness, reconnecting with our innate essence, and relinquishing the elements that foster the illusion of our detachment from the greater whole of existence.

"Guidelines for Engaging in Chakra Alignment Meditation: "

Please take a seat: It is necessary for you to locate a serene and comfortable environment, completely devoid of any disturbances. This holds particular significance for individuals who are inexperienced in the discipline. Ultimately, you have the ability to accomplish it from any location of your choosing.

Close your eyes: Ensure that you are positioned in a comfortable manner and proceed to calmly and serenely shut your eyes. Direct your attention to your breath, enabling it to remain in its current state, devoid of any alteration. Over time, it is probable that you will observe a gradual deceleration and deepening of your breath without any conscious effort. Allow it to unfold organically without passing judgment on the unfolding events. Respiring is the most innate action within the human experience.

Remain Mindful: The utmost crucial element of this meditation entails ensuring that your attention remains steadfast on your breath, diligently redirecting any wandering thoughts to a state of calmness. It is probable that your mind will tend to stray during this activity, which is entirely normal. Upon observing this, refrain from reprimanding or passing judgment upon oneself. Initially, it is recommended to engage in brief intervals of this activity, commencing with a duration of five minutes. As soon as you experience a sense of ease, gradually progress towards extended durations of seated engagement.

The Interplay of Respiration as a Link and Manifestation of the Ethereal:

Given that we exist within the realm of the physical, the act of breathing and its interconnectedness with air may be considered as the most immediate embodiment of the spiritual realm. By accessing this innate activity and directing our attention towards our personal experience, we are accessing a sense of appreciation for our existence. Upon commencing this endeavor, on a daily basis (preferably), it will become evident that your thoughts frequently stray. While this is acceptable, it is imperative that you consciously acknowledge and redirect your attention to the meditation whenever such occurrences arise, maintaining a composed demeanor. Once you acquaint yourself with the rhythm of this practice, you will attain a state of serenity and tranquility, recognizing your interconnectedness within the larger context.

This particular chakra is commonly known as the "root or support" chakra, and can be found positioned at the base of the spinal cord within the coccygeal region. This is suggested by the depiction of a lotus adorned with four petals of a vibrant red hue. It embodies the energetic center associated with ensuring personal safety, instinctual wisdom, steadfastness, and fundamental human capabilities. Mulahdhara is responsible for governing matters pertaining to spirituality, sexuality, security, and sensuality. When the root chakra is unblocked, an individual experiences a sense of stability and security. The emotional concerns that have a tendency to impact Mulahdhara primarily pertain to matters of survival, encompassing aspects such as finance, sustenance, and achieving financial autonomy.

SVADHISTHANA

The sacral chakra, often known as the center of sexuality and creativity, is the designated term for this specific chakra. The Svadhisthana energy center is situated in the vicinity of the lower abdominal region. It can be characterized as a white lotus featuring six orange petals or vermillion enclosed within a crescent moon shape. The Svadhishthana chakra is situated in the sacrum region and is thought to align with the reproductive organs, namely the ovaries and testes, which produce the multiple sex hormones implicated in the reproductive cycle. This particular chakra exercises dominion over matters of reproduction, artistic expressions, delight, and fervor. The challenges connected with this particular chakra encompass aggression, gratification, fundamental emotional necessities, and dependencies.

MANIPURA

This particular chakra serves as the origin of individual empowerment; it is positioned in the vicinity of the navel, extending up to the sternum. This particular chakra is represented by a downward-pointing triangle adorned with ten petals of a vibrant yellow color. This particular chakra facilitates the development of self-assurance and the ability to maintain personal composure. The emotional challenges linked to Manipura encompass anxiety, apprehension, authority, self-reflection, among others. This chakra exercises control over the processes of digestion, individual potency, and various aspects pertaining to development.

ANAHATA

The "heart" chakra is commonly recognized to symbolize sentiments of love, compassion, and benevolence. It is located centrally within the thoracic region, specifically at the sternum. It serves as the conduit through which the spiritual realm and the physical realm are interconnected. Anahata is represented by a floral structure of circular shape, exhibiting a set of twelve verdant petals. This chakra holds dominion over matters of ardor, dedication, the flow of energy, and the unconditional affection harbored towards oneself and others. The matters pertaining to this chakra encompass feelings of being excluded, intricate emotional states, as well as delicate sensibilities.

VISHUDDA

This chakra is commonly designated as the "throat" chakra and is situated in the throat region, including the thyroid, tongue, and mouth. This particular chakra is denoted by a silver crescent encompassed within a white circular form, accompanied by a constellation of sixteen petals in a delicate shade of celestial blue. It regulates the process of communication, fosters autonomy, facilitates coherent thinking, and promotes a feeling of safety. When the Vishudda is insufficiently stimulated, an individual may exhibit introversion or shyness, while excessive stimulation of this energy center can result in talkativeness and poor listening skills.

AJNA

The chakra known as the "third eye" is characterized by a lotus containing two petals, traditionally depicted as white in color. It pertains to the acquisition of insights, perceptual awareness, and meticulousness at an intuitive dimension. The matters related to this chakra encompass placing trust in internal guidance and aligning the higher and lower aspects of oneself in a state of harmony.

SAHASRARA

It is commonly identified as the "crown" chakra, situated at the apex of the head or superior to the crown area. The embodiment of this particular chakra is symbolized through the white lotus with a profusion of one thousand vibrant petals. The Sahasrara chakra presides over the faculties of contemplation, harmony, and existence. When Sahasrara is in a state of reduced activity, individuals exhibit a lack of awareness regarding spirituality and a rigidity in their thinking. Conversely, when the chakra is excessively active, individuals tend to disregard bodily desires and prioritize spiritual matters.

Attaining Chakra Healing And Activation Via Simplified And Pragmatic Measures

One can employ diverse techniques to facilitate the restoration of harmony and equilibrium within the chakras. Nutritious dietary substances, medicinal herbs, and even the application of essential oils possess the potential to facilitate the enhancement of one's chakra's well-being. In subsequent chapters, we shall discuss alternative approaches such as the integration of auditory stimuli, the utilization of yogic practices, the application of meditative techniques, and the employment of positive affirmations. However, for the present moment, we will adhere to the more pragmatic methodologies.

Essential Oils

In the forthcoming chapters, we will delve into the utilization of essential oils in facilitating the process of healing and harmonizing the chakras. For comprehensive guidance regarding the utilization of aromatherapy or essential oils, it is advised to gently apply a quantity of 1-3 drops of the mixture onto the designated energy center. As an illustrative example, should one seek to restore balance to the Root Chakra, it is recommended to gently administer the concoction to the area situated at the fundament of the spinal column. In addition, it is optimal to perform this anointing during your designated meditation sessions. Regarding the aforementioned ratio, you are at liberty to employ the rule that allocates 30% to the top oil, 50% to the middle oil, and 20% to the base oil.

Effective Methods for Balancing the Root Chakra:

Wearing red clothes

Engaging in lower body exercises such as walking and jogging, as well as including sexual activity, is advisable for physical fitness.

Grounding: engaging in the practice of walking without footwear on natural terrain.

Massages; you will additionally reap advantages from administering massages.

Expressing gratitude for your blessings, such as offering a blessing for the food you are about to consume.

Consume the following foods: tofu, eggs, soy, beets, beans, meat, parsnips.

An amalgamation of fundamental oils: sandalwood, cedar wood, patchouli, rosemary, and myrrh

Opening the Root Chakra:

Activating the Root Chakra is not as arduous as one might envision. To begin with, implementing the aforementioned techniques will already alleviate the obstruction; however, to optimize the efficacy, it is advised to assume a standing position with feet slightly apart for a brief duration. This is the posture that facilitates the establishment of stable foundation. It is also recommended to engage in recreational strolls amidst natural surroundings. The additional measure you must undertake is the cultivation of mindfulness. As you are stationary or in motion, remain fully present and refrain from dwelling on the past or anticipating the future.

Effective Remedies for Balancing the Sacral Chakra:

Hydrating yourself

Engaging in outdoor activities and immersing oneself in the natural environment, particularly bodies of water including oceans, lakes, rivers, and streams.

Consume the following food items: oranges, coconuts, melons, and various other succulent fruits.

Proprietary blend of essential oils comprising blue chamomile, neroli, ylang ylang, and clary sage

Opening the Sacral Chakra:

To restore the proper functioning of an obstructed chakra, one might consider engaging in the practice of dancing, as it facilitates enhanced energy circulation and vitality. Furthermore, it is recommended to engage in hip-opening exercises. Donning and observing anything of an orange hue can also alleviate the obstruction. If you perceive a significant burden of thoughts on your mind, consider alleviating them by means of expressive writing in a journal.

Effective Methods for Restoring Balance to the Solar Plexus Chakra:

Exposing oneself to sunlight.

Engage in public speaking exercises - simulate an audience by positioning yourself opposite a wall or mirror and envisioning a crowd before you.

Participating in seminars or forums focused on the subject of personal growth and self-improvement

Consume the following food items: yellow-hued foods such as bananas, cheese, yellow peppers, golden apples, brown rice, oats, sweet potatoes, and pumpkins.

The mixture of essential oils consists of frankincense, rosemary, lemongrass, and roman chamomile.

Activating the Solar Plexus Chakra:

Gaining access to the third energy center can prove to be challenging, particularly in the case of a longstanding blockage. It may require a greater investment of time and exertion, nevertheless, it is plausible to achieve through the implementation of the strategies delineated in the segment pertaining to Practical Methods for Restoring the Solar Plexus Chakra.

Effective Techniques for the Restoration of the Heart Chakra:

Maintain a personal record to document all the positive aspects that come your way.

Adorning garments in the hues of green or pink.

When you have accomplished commendable tasks, it is essential to acknowledge your efforts and grant yourself a reward.

Participate in endeavors that promote cardiovascular well-being, such as volunteering or engaging in recreational activities with animals.

Doing deep breathing exercises

Consume these food items: verdant vegetables such as broccoli, kale, cabbage, and collard greens.

Utilize this indispensable amalgamation of essential oils: rose, ylang ylang, sandalwood, and roman chamomile.

Opening the Heart Chakra:

In contrast to the preceding three energy domains, the activation of the Heart Chakra necessitates a greater degree of individual resolve. Why? Removing the obstruction necessitates a comprehensive comprehension of one's own self. Commence by recognizing the multifaceted nature of your existence, signifying the presence of numerous roles that contribute to your overall being. Embrace them and undoubtedly, display affection towards them. Through the implementation of this approach, the internal conflicts will be effectively resolved, leading to a gradual development of greater compassion and understanding towards oneself.

Effective Methods for Restoring Balance to the Throat Chakra:

Engaging in soothing endeavors involving your vocal cords, such as gently vocalizing, participating in melodic expression, and reciting rhythmic phrases.

Wearing blue clothes

Engaging in outdoor activities and observing the cloud formations.

Conventional physical activities such as Qui Gong and Tai Chi

Documenting your emotions and/or attentively receiving perspectives from others.

Engaging in the activity of delivering speeches in front of a wall or mirror.

Gargling with salt water

Consume the following food items: lemon, grapefruit, lime, herbal teas, kiwi, apricots, plums.

Kindly employ this crucial combination of essential oils: lavender, tea tree, and rose geranium.

Opening the Throat Chakra:

In addition to the aforementioned methods, the following approaches may be employed to unblock the Throat Chakra: purify the environment through the utilization of aromatherapy (utilizing a blend of calendula, ylang ylang, rosemary, and jasmine), engaging in candid discussions with a trusted confidant or family member regarding one's concerns, engaging in journaling as a means of introspection, maintaining proper hydration, and relinquishing attachments to circumstances beyond one's control or the ability to remedy.

Effective Methods for Balancing and Restoring the Third Eye Chakra:

Administering camphor topically to the region corresponding to the Third Eye Chakra during nighttime.

Prayer/Meditation

Positive visualization

Reading

Consume the following food items: foods of a purple hue, such as eggplant, blueberries, plum, purple cabbage, and kale.

Utilize this essential oil combination consisting of sandalwood, clary sage, lavender, marjoram, and rosemary.

Activating the Ajna Chakra:

The human mind possesses immense potential in terms of harmonizing and unblocking the third eye chakra. A favorable perspective, constructive mental imagery, and mindful contemplation hold significant importance.

Effective Approaches to Balancing the Crown Chakra:

Please adhere to the dress code and choose attire in the shades of violet, gold, and white.

Praying

Breathing exercises

Meditation (most powerful method)

Consume the following foods: organically grown produce, recipes for juice cleansing, as they are beneficial for physical detoxification.

Utilize this vital amalgamation of essential oils: angelica wood, frankincense, myrrh, jasmine, and cedar wood.

Opening the Crown Chakra:

In order to unblock the Crown chakra, it is imperative to seek a tranquil environment as a primary step. It is possible to accomplish it in any location. Consider exploring your bedroom or taking a leisurely stroll in a serene park as alternative options. During moments of quietude, it is possible to employ the affirmations that will be expounded upon subsequently, in conjunction with the meditation methods that shall be bestowed upon you.

The Chakra associated with the Solar Plexus

The Solar Plexus Chakra is alternatively referred to as the Navel Chakra due to its physical location within the region of the navel. It exerts influence over our level of self-assurance and capacity for success. It is the underlying impetus that continues to propel us forward. It compels us to actively pursue transformation and effectuate constructive changes in our own lives, while concurrently facilitating the uplifting transformation of others. It goes without saying that confidence is undeniably one of the fundamental factors contributing to achieving success. It compels us to embrace emerging opportunities instead of succumbing to apprehension and resistance towards change. Hence, the Solar Plexus Chakra holds a significant position among the seven primary Chakras.

For individuals who are compelled to inquire about the factors impeding their progress or hindering their personal growth, it is highly probable that an imbalance in the Solar Plexus Chakra could provide the explanation. The aforementioned difficulties may pertain to a deficiency in focus and self-assurance. Furthermore, the occurrence of underperformance in a specific situation can be attributed to the influence of the Solar Plexus Chakra. Inability to effectively communicate and diminished self-confidence are additional manifestations of an underactive state of this Chakra. When discussing the naval, it symbolizes the focal point of the human body and serves as the gravitational nexus of connection. The central region possesses superior core strength as it efficiently channels and disperses energy throughout the entirety of the physique. This is why in order to possess a robust physical foundation, it is imperative to cultivate a resilient navel Chakra or Solar Plexus Chakra.

Fortifying this Chakra is akin to fortifying the optimal core. The endeavor enhances our self-assurance, thus leading to improved physical well-being. Observe the upright stance we adopt, which exemplifies a commendable posture that conveys confidence through the effective use of body language. It is commonly recognized that a robust mental state is directly correlated with physical strength; conversely, when one's mental faculties are feeble, physical vitality tends to wane accordingly. Consequently, it is imperative to enhance the core and engage in exercises that fortify the Solar Plexus Chakra.

The optimal method for achieving equilibrium in the Solar Plexus Chakra involves engaging in actions that bolster self-assurance. Specifically, garnering significant attention may evoke feelings of discomfort or unease. However, consider the illustration of a president delivering a speech to the entire nation, who effectively accomplishes this task with utmost proficiency. It is imperative that his Solar Plexus Chakra maintains a robust and unwavering level of energy.

Additionally, it can be asserted with considerable self-regard and high self-worth, akin to the satisfaction one derives from self-reflection. This occurs when one adorns oneself in attire that aligns with personal preferences, rather than solely seeking to appease others. That method is the most optimal means to enhance the vitality of this particular Chakra. Confidence is paramount, and it is imperative to take this into consideration. Adopting the correct path, engaging in purposeful pursuits, and cultivating your determination, among other factors, will enhance your self-assurance. These factors can contribute to the development of assertiveness in an individual.

In the event of an imbalance or obstruction occurring in your Solar Plexus Chakra, you may experience sensations of peril, provocation, and apprehension. This is an obstructed Chakra, resulting in a sense of powerlessness. You may encounter adverse emotions and develop a sense of inferiority. It is plausible that you may begin to perceive that the world is harboring animosity towards you. There exist internal barriers impeding your progress and hindering your ability to advance.

However, it should be noted that an excessively active Solar Plexus Chakra may manifest in one's actions being carried out in an authoritarian manner. You possess a relentless pursuit for perfection so as to render it unattainable, when you are akin to those who share this trait. Due to this factor, you may experience an increased desire or a perpetual sense of insufficiency. Additionally, you develop a strong desire for authority. You aspire for authority with the intention of exerting influence over individuals according to your desires. It is probable that you will exercise stringent judgment and criticism towards individuals, displaying excessive self-assurance that may ultimately contribute to your detriment. The above mentioned indicators are indicative of an excessively active Solar Plexus Chakra. Therefore, it is imperative to acquire the knowledge and techniques necessary to restore equilibrium to this chakra before the situation exacerbates further.

Position: The Solar Plexus Chakra is situated inferior to the chest, between the navel and ribcage. It resides in the core of your physique, akin to the commanding core of Ironman.

Color Attribute: It is linked to the hue yellow, which represents the manifestation of light.

Sangkrit: It is referred to as Manipura in the Sanskrit language.

The bedrock of this Chakra revolves around wisdom and authority. That is the manner in which it reacts to the cognitive and physical capabilities of an individual. Additionally, it requires the bravery to release ego and maintain one's self-worth.

The embodiment of strength and self-assurance is exhibited through the warrior posture, depicting the yogic position and mantra associated with this particular Chakra. To properly execute the mantra, interlock your thumbs with your fingers, ensuring they come into contact with one another. Proceed by positioning your hand between the region encompassing your heart and abdomen. Furthermore, we offer Yoga-compatible crystals designed to enhance your self-assurance; we recommend considering citrine point and sulfur crystals for this purpose. In order to channel your attention towards or activate your Solar Plexus Chakra, you may opt to either adorn it or grasp it firmly.

In order to achieve equilibrium in this considerable energy, it is essential to first discern the indicators of its constructive effects on your physique. It can bolster self-assurance when one is cognizant of their aspirations and finds tranquility in aligning their life with purpose. You cultivate a positive disposition and consistently strive to enhance your self-image, avoiding stagnation and embracing growth.

Additional indicators of a blocked or imbalanced state of this particular Chakra can be observed in individuals experiencing feelings of shame, as well as a tendency to consistently lower their gaze, thereby inhibiting their ability to maintain proper eye contact. One's sense of direction in life becomes lost; a lack of clarity about the path to pursue and a tendency towards diminished self-worth are observed. Consequently, the diminished energy flux emanating from the Solar Plexus Chakra will incline individuals towards indecisiveness, thereby impeding their ability to enhance their life circumstances.

You adopt the role of a target to your own mind due to the persistent tendency to excessively ruminate and be overly concerned with numerous superfluous matters. On the contrary, excessive stimulation of the Solar Plexus Chakra elicits an overactive response characterized by tendencies towards perfectionism and a desire for excessive attention. Such individuals may display an undue propensity for excessive criticism of insignificant matters, accompanied by a lack of self-control leading to frequent difficulties. Additionally, trust issues may arise, potentially accompanied by an insatiable hunger for power.

In order to establish equilibrium within the Solar Plexus Chakra and uphold its harmonious and advantageous condition, one must exercise control over their respiration. A sizable number of individuals engage in shallow, chest-oriented breathing, which fails to fully encompass our entire lung capacity with optimal efficiency. If one is inhaling through the nasal passage, it is advisable to acquire the technique of abdominal or diaphragmatic breathing. Utilizing diaphragmatic breathing enables one to effectively expand their lung capacity, facilitating the intake of vital oxygen into the body. This process aids in the purification of both mind and body by eliminating harmful toxins. Maintain a consistent and regulated breath in order to provide your body with a consistent and uninterrupted supply of oxygen. Additionally, it is crucial to allocate a secure environment permeated with fresh air, as this will facilitate the release of any blockages within your Solar Plexus Chakra.

In accordance with its vibrant yellow hue, one simply requires the presence of sunlight. However, it is imperative to ascertain the appropriate moments to bask in its radiance and when to seek respite from it. Remain exposed to sunlight, albeit for a limited duration. One may also observe the propensity for individuals to exhibit an affinity for donning attire in hues of yellow, displaying an affection for this particular color. Consequently, they exude an aura of cheerfulness and self-assurance, thereby establishing a notable presence. You have the opportunity to adopt this style of clothing and enjoy the advantages that come with the hue of yellow. This outcome can be attributed to the enhancement of the Solar Plexus Chakra, which elicits a sense of joy and contentment in individuals. In terms of enhancing this particular Chakra, I would recommend incorporating nourishing fruits such as bananas or other yellow-hued food items like an omelet into your diet. An alternative approach entails embracing the process of respiration, as previously indicated, by making use of the aromas emanating from bergamot, cypress, jasmine, or geranium. It will foster a state of tranquility for both your psychological and physiological well-being.

The Heart Chakra

The cardiovascular system is deemed critical within the human anatomy. Amputating any part of your body, such as your leg, arm, or hand, will lead to incapacitation rather than immediate fatality. Alternatively, removing your heart would also result in the cessation of your existence. The Heart Chakra pertains to the emotional energies associated with yearning, affection, and benevolence. When discussing the concept of desire, it is the driving force behind our vigorous endeavors to attain our desired objectives in life. Nevertheless, the inclination towards materialism, perfectionism, or any form of self-centered gratification will ultimately deceive us, rather than genuinely aiding our personal growth and development. Consequently, this will give rise to the attenuation of the Heart Chakra, which could potentially impact our psychological state.

Insufficient vitality within the Heart Chakra diminishes the presence of favorable energy within your being. This culminates in an incapacity to exert control over one's own mental faculties, thereby exerting a detrimental impact on one's innermost longings. How would one identify the manifestations of energy deficiency? One might encounter individuals who choose to remain insular, internalizing their challenges and refraining from expressing their thoughts and viewpoints. They exhibit a propensity to excessively analyze and complicate their lives, thus inadvertently subjecting themselves to unnecessary stress. Ultimately, this can result in the development of depressive symptoms. In summary, the disequilibrium of the Heart Chakra may give rise to an unhealthy state of mind.

Additionally, it is imperative to bear in mind that the heart perpetually contracts and relaxes in order to propel oxygenated and nutrient-rich blood to every region of our anatomy. Consequently, as the cardiac muscle loses strength, the body's blood circulation is correspondingly diminished. In the event of such occurrence, the body will be deprived of the requisite sustenance vital for its sustenance. This can potentially give rise to complications in various other bodily regions.

This principle can be extended to encompass our aspirations and cognitive faculties as well. If we were to consider a scenario in which our minds are devoid of proper aspirations and instead foster negative inclinations, it is to be expected that we would encounter a decline in physical well-being and vitality, stemming from an inadequate intake of nourishment. To restore equilibrium within the Heart Chakra, it is imperative to acknowledge both the unfavorable and favorable inclinations residing within our thoughts, and subsequently relinquish the detrimental desires that perpetually amass, encompassing excessive displays of emotions, incessant pursuit of flawlessness, or establishment of impracticable standards. Furthermore, it is imperative to maintain adherence to your positive aspirations, such as fostering humility and striving towards accomplishing your life objectives.

In addition to the longing, the Heart Chakra pertains to the concepts of unwavering love, benevolence, and receptiveness. The customary equilibrium factors for this particular Chakra encompass sentiments such as love, benevolence, absolution, receptiveness, gratitude, and serenity.

The obstruction of the Heart Chakra entails the presence of bitterness or resentment stemming from one's interference in either their own life or the lives of others. In addition, it encompasses a dearth of empathy and an unwillingness to accept or cherish love and connections.

The intermediate state between equilibrium and disequilibrium is characterized by the heightened influence of the Heart Chakra, reflecting an excessive allocation of energy that may result in self-sacrifice or an excessive reliance on others, whereby one prioritizes the needs of others at the expense of one's own well-being. This continuous pattern of sacrifice may eventually lead to personal loss and a diminished sense of self. Furthermore, it is possible that you may not attain a sense of independence or discover an environment that allows you to express your true self, which can be compounded by excessive jealousy within the confines of the relationship.

Furthermore, it is a prevailing occurrence for individuals to adopt an emotionally guarded demeanor following the dissolution of their romantic relationships. It can be asserted that they harbor a fear towards love and apprehension when it comes to making additional commitments. When such a situation arises, individuals who possess a well-balanced Heart Chakra will possess the wisdom to maintain composure and commence the process of healing their wounded heart. It implies that they are able to progress more expediently, refraining from expending their time on a dissolved previous affiliation. They possess an understanding of the underlying cause, and exhibit a more sound state of mind when contemplating the factors that contributed to the deterioration and ultimate dissolution of their relationship.

Conversely, individuals with a deficient Heart Chakra may find themselves immobile, unable to progress, consumed by pessimism, and ensnared by emotional distress, subsequently harboring profound sorrow. This would effectively extinguish their inner vitality. Regarding the state of emotional numbness, it is a widely recognized consequence among individuals who have encountered a succession of romantic separations, setbacks, shortcomings, and disillusionments. These sentiments exemplify the emotions that we must make a concerted effort to steer clear of, lest they engulf us entirely, even though it may appear alluring to indulge in the depths of these emotions. Instances of emotional distress can significantly affect the Heart Chakra, leading to an intensified immersion into pessimism and negativity. It will also have an impact on your physical presentation. You will appear pallid, disheveled, and emotionally ravaged.

Achieving Chakra Healing Via The Practice Of Mindful Existence

The restoration of harmony in your chakras has the potential to alleviate your physical ailments. Since you possess ultimate control over the energy you generate, albeit in a challenging manner, you possess the capability to restore your own well-being. It is imperative to consider that the energy one generates contributes to the flow of energy within their chakras, thereby influencing their state of balance. This emotional energy frequently manifests in physical symptoms such as pain, causing discomfort. If left unattended, these symptoms can escalate into illness and reach an intolerable state.

After gaining a general understanding of the source of your imbalance, the initial step to take is to embark on the practice of cultivating mindfulness. This may be delineated as existing in a perpetual state of mindfulness, characterized by a profound awareness of one's self, one's environment, and one's cognitive state. What is the method of transportation to arrive at the desired destination?

A meditative practice serves as a strong basis for cultivating a state of mindful existence. There exist several distinct meditation techniques that can be employed for each individual chakra. These meditations can serve as a foundation. Each chakra is accompanied by a corresponding mantra sound, diligently employed during meditation to facilitate the restoration of its corresponding chakra. Meditation plays a crucial role in maintaining optimal chakra well-being. To restore balance to your chakras, it is imperative that you integrate the practice of meditation into your daily routine. While it may appear intimidating for individuals with limited experience, it is important to note that it does not necessitate a significant investment of time. It is highly recommended to invest a considerable amount of effort into your meditation practice as the results you achieve are directly proportional to the level of dedication and commitment you apply.

If you have not previously experienced the state of meditation, there is no need for concern. The state of meditation is contingent upon one's viewpoint. The aforementioned process varies from individual to individual, and one will undertake it in a manner distinct to their own, which may not necessarily align with the approaches of others. It entails directing one's mental attention internally. Typically, this activity is performed in a seated posture, with the legs positioned in a crossed manner. Please make an effort to conceptualize your thoughts more objectively. Establish a purpose for your meditative endeavor, specifically aiming to restore the chakra of your choice and promote overall vitality within all of the chakras. You have the option to either sway gently or remain seated in a stationary position. You might consider maintaining a stationary position initially, and then gradually introduce a rocking motion. Maintaining proper posture and alignment of the spine is of utmost significance, particularly during the practice of meditation intended to harmonize the chakras. Position your hands in a manner where the palms are facing downwards and rest them gently upon your knees. Ensure that you take deep and regular breaths, allowing your exhales to be twice as long in duration as your inhales. Directing your attention towards your breath will facilitate the process of calming and purging your mind of distractions. After attaining a state of deep respiration, engage in the recitation of the mantra associated with the targeted chakra for the purpose of healing. Ultimately, your mentation will become lucid, facilitating entry into a state of meditative transcendence.

Exercises for activating the root chakra.

For the purpose of this meditation, assume a seated posture outdoors. It is imperative to maintain physical contact with the earth, as the root chakra serves as the foundational energy center that fosters a sense of connection and groundedness to the natural world. Please proceed by closing your eyes, arranging your legs in a crossed position, and attaining a state of meditation. During the course of your meditation, it is recommended that you engage in the recitation of the designated sound associated with the chakra, namely, LAM. One can draw upon the essence of this word in each breath, thereby reestablishing a profound connection to the fundamental source of this chakra and nurturing a stronger bond with both the earthly realm and one's own physical vessel.

An additional measure that can aid in harmonizing your root chakra is engaging in kegel exercises. Furthermore, engaging in specific yoga postures can aid in restoring equilibrium to your root chakra. This chakra serves the purpose of providing stability and can be enhanced through the practice of grounding yoga poses, which can prove to be beneficial. Grounding postures encompass poses that involve extensive contact between various parts of the body and the ground. A selection of these stances comprises:

Squat Position, also known as Malasana. In the present posture, one must firmly position their feet on the ground while bending their knees into a squatting position. This action brings about an inclination of your pelvic floor in the direction of the ground, thereby facilitating unimpeded circulation of energy through the chakra.

• The posture known as Padmasana, also referred to as the Lotus pose. In this position, the feet are positioned over the contralateral thighs. Lotus pose offers a more intensified stretch compared to a cross-legged position, while also being slightly more challenging. Over time, you may also adopt the lotus position for the purpose of meditation. The practice of assuming the lotus positions results in a complete grounding of both the physical and mental aspects within your being. It has the ability to impede the circulation of adverse energy or energy that has become destabilized, thereby moderating the influx of excessive energy within this particular domain.

• The first posture is known as the Mountain pose, also referred to as Tadasana. Ensure that your feet are steadfast on the ground and stretch out your arms laterally, with your palms directed outward. This particular posture holds significant importance, not only for the root chakra, but also for the holistic healing of all the chakras. By facilitating alignment of these energy centers along the spine, it fosters a state of energetic wellness within the various systems.

Sacral chakra exercise

For the purpose of this meditation, individuals have the option to either position themselves outdoors or retreat to an enclosed, chilled environment while maintaining distance from others. You have the option to assume a cross-legged sitting position or alternatively, stand. Commence the regulation of your respiration and endeavor to attain a contemplative state by intoning the designated mantra associated with this particular chakra, specifically the resonant utterance of VAM. The auditory stimulus will contribute to the regulation of energy in this vicinity, though should you prefer, you may also engage in a visualization exercise. To facilitate the influx of energy towards the sacral chakra, envision its directed flow towards that particular location. Visualizing the vibrant hue of orange as a dynamic aura, ascending from the earth and ultimately settling within your sacral chakra, integrating and assimilating harmoniously.

To foster equilibrium in your sacral chakra, it is essential to cultivate sentiments of affection and benevolence within the realm of your intimate connections. An alternative approach would be to employ the breathing technique known as Ida Nadi, whereby you gently occlude the right nostril and then proceed to take a deep inhalation through the left nostril. Engage in this activity for a duration of ten breaths, thereafter discontinuing. Ida Nadi serves as a conduit of energy that specifically nourishes the sacral chakra, predominantly benefiting women due to its inherent lunar qualities. Nonetheless, abstaining from it is not recommended for the male demographic. Engaging in this practice is highly advantageous for individuals of all genders and can be undertaken either prior to or following the meditative session.

Yoga postures that can be performed to enhance the equilibrium of your sacral chakra encompass different asanas that engage in the activation and reinforcement of the muscles located in the pelvic floor and pubic area.

Supta Baddha Konasana, alternatively referred to as the butterfly pose, followed by a seated forward bend. Assume a seated posture with your feet in close proximity, allowing your knees to naturally separate outward. They have the potential to come into contact with the ground, but it is not guaranteed. Bend at the waist, bringing your hips forward and positioning your head between your knees. This posture facilitates the synchronization of the sacral chakra through the elongation of the pelvic floor.

• Bhujangasana, commonly referred to as the cobra pose. This posture is achieved by exerting pressure on the floor with the body, resulting in the elevation of the head and shoulders. The hands possess the ability to reside either adjacent to the body or pressed firmly against the Earth's surface. Engage your hip muscles by firmly applying pressure to the ground in this manner. It effectively works to establish a strong foundation for the sacral chakra.

• Parivrtta Trikonasana, also known as the pose of twisted triangle, involves the rotation of the torso while assuming the triangle pose, accompanied by turning the head and shoulders accordingly. This motion facilitates hip opening, enabling the reception of positive energy while stimulating your creative faculty. Additionally, the twisting action aids in the expulsion of negative energy.

Training regimen for the warrior energy center.

For the purpose of this meditation, you have the option to be situated in a room with elevated temperature or alternatively, exposed to natural sunlight outdoors. Ensure that the temperature is not excessively high, as it may hinder your ability to concentrate. However, it is noteworthy that warmth tends to attract the specific energy required by your warrior chakra. The designated chant pertaining to this specific chakra is the resonating utterance of RAM. Utilize this sound as a means to channel and attract vital energy towards this particular realm. During the practice of meditation, direct your attention towards the sense of inner buoyancy. Envision the transmission of energy towards your third chakra.

Following the meditation session, assume a posture with an upright spine and engage in the intentional act of inhaling and exhaling with abbreviated breaths. Please respire by means of your nasal passages rather than utilizing your oral cavity. Subsequently, exert a strong inhalation while simultaneously extending the abdominal area outward. When exhaling, exerting force, retract your abdominal muscles towards your spine. Inhale rapidly and engage the entirety of your core musculature to contract and expand your abdominal region. Inhale and exhale in this manner for a duration of ten breaths, followed by a pause of four breaths. I recommend iterating this procedure several times. You will experience a discernible surge of vitality, manifesting as a comforting sensation of warmth and subtle muscular stimulation in your warrior chakra. This practice is commonly referred to as Bhastrika Breath. This will provide a significant boost of energy to this particular area, revitalizing your chakra system. Additionally, it will facilitate the process of digestion and enhance metabolic rates.

Yoga poses for the warrior chakra are the poses which strengthen and widen the area of your solar plexus:

- The first asana in the sequence is Virabhadrasana 1, commonly referred to as Warrior One. Assume a wide-legged stance with the right foot positioned forward in a lunge. Both feet are oriented anteriorly, with the rear one rotated outward. Flex the leading knee to execute the lunge and adopt your preferred arm positioning. Play around with it. This stance facilitates the redirection of energy, particularly towards the third chakra, promoting the harmonious circulation of energy throughout the entire chakra system.

- Undertake the Dhanurasana or Boat pose by assuming a prone position and flexing your knees. Elevate your chest from the ground while extending your arms posteriorly to grasp onto your feet. Retract your lower extremities while employing your upper limbs to exert force. You may engage in gentle swaying movements while assuming this position, directing the flow of energy towards the area encompassing the solar plexus chakra.

Engage in exercises aimed at developing the energy flow of the heart chakra.

During this contemplation, it is advisable to locate oneself indoors within a tranquil environment. As you inhale, kindly direct your focus towards your thoracic region, and take measures to broaden it sufficiently, thereby facilitating the utmost openness of your cardiac area. The prescribed practice for focusing on the heart chakra during meditation involves chanting the mantra

"YUM." Therefore, deliberately inhale this particular word to facilitate the infusion of revitalizing energy into the heart chakra. Maintain a pleasant countenance while engaging in meditation. It possesses the capacity to facilitate the release of the precise form of energy necessary to navigate effectively in society. Furthermore, should you willingly bestow this energy to others, it shall inevitably be returned to you.

The yoga postures intended for the heart chakra primarily encompass heart-opening poses, incorporating asanas aimed at expanding the chest and directing energy towards this specific region.

• Practicing Ustrasana, also known as the Camel pose, involves assuming a kneeling position with a properly aligned spine, ensuring optimal alignment of all chakras. Inhale deeply, allowing your chest to expand while simultaneously extending your hands backwards, ensuring to engage your core muscles in order to maintain stability and prevent any likelihood of losing balance in a backwards direction. You may opt to position your hands on your lower back, or alternatively, you can extend downwards and secure your ankles. Your chest should be completely open to receive energy to the heart chakra.

• Perform Setu Bandha Sarvangasana, also known as bridge pose: Assume a supine position with your knees flexed at a triangular angle and the soles of your feet firmly planted on the floor. While taking a breath, elevate your hips and suspend them above the ground. If it is your preference, you may opt to extend your chest forward in order to enhance the flow of energy in this particular posture. The bridge pose is highly effective in the dissipation of negative energy as well.

Bhujangasana, commonly known as cobra pose, serves as an excellent means to open and energize the heart, constituting an integral component of a comprehensive yoga regimen. Assume a supine position with your arms flexed and the palms of your hands resting on the floor adjacent to either your shoulders or chest area. As you engage in the act of inhalation, lengthen your spinal column (bringing those chakras into proper alignment!) and elevate your countenance and thorax away from the surface. It is recommended that you release your breath and recline on the floor once again. Repeat this several time. This is a dynamic sequence that serves to attract positive energy while simultaneously dispelling negative energy through the integration of controlled breathing and purposeful movement.

Exercise for the fifth chakra

Commence by occupying a tranquil environment. Given that this particular chakra pertains to communication in various forms, including verbal and symbolic expression, it is imperative for you to intone the mantra: YUM. The act of engaging in physical movements and audibly reciting or even melodiously uttering the mantra has the potential to alleviate any energy blockages present in the throat region. Furthermore, the harmonious resonance produced by singing shall attract positive energy towards oneself.

One may also engage in the practice of Lion Breath to promote the circulation of energy towards the throat chakra. This particular pranayama technique offers a pleasurable experience while effectively alleviating stress and dispelling negative energy accumulations. Please inhale deeply, expanding your lungs more than ever before, and contract your facial muscles by narrowing your eyes, nose, and mouth, creating a resemblance to a raisin. Subsequently, exhale forcefully in one go, allowing your facial muscles to release tension and extending your tongue as far out of your mouth as possible. Perform this action a maximum of ten repetitions.

The yoga postures targeting the throat chakra encompass those that work to activate and invigorate the throat and thyroid glands.

• Salamba Sarvangasana, also known as the Shoulder Stand, facilitates the focalization of energy towards the throat chakra. Assume a supine position and transition into bridge pose. While positioned on the bridge, support your lower back by placing your hands underneath it and initiate a movement by propelling yourself away from the floor with a kicking motion. Elevate your legs to a 90-degree angle with the floor. It is recommended that you assume a shoulder stand position. If you possess the necessary strength and inclination, you may choose to release your hands from supporting your lower back and place them on the ground. Please maintain this posture for as long as possible, but refrain from exceeding a duration of three minutes as it may have adverse effects beyond that point.

- Halasana or Plow Pose provides heightened activation of the throat chakra compared to Shoulder Stand. Transitioning from shoulder stand (it is essential to initiate this pose by placing your hands beneath your lower back) gradually and cautiously elongate your legs in the posterior direction. It is possible for them to be either in a state of suspension in the air or in contact with the ground at shoulder level. Please maintain this posture for a duration not exceeding one minute to achieve optimal outcomes.

Engage in exercises for the third eye energy center.

This is a contemplative technique that can be performed with eyes either open or closed. However, for individuals who are new to the practice of meditation, closing the eyes may offer greater convenience. During the act of meditation, direct your utmost focus and energy towards the location known as the third eye, positioned above the line of your eyebrows and between your two physical eyes. Reiterate the mantra SHAM within your consciousness while concentrating your vitality and engaging in deliberate and meticulous breath control, reminiscent of customary meditative practices. If an individual experiences sensations in the region corresponding to their third eye, it can be interpreted as a positive indication.

Appropriate asanas for cultivating the third eye involve postures that are understated, contemplative, and tranquil. Typically, they direct their attention inward.

- Balasana, alternatively known as Child's Pose, is a highly accessible yoga posture that can be comfortably performed in any location. Assume a kneeling position with gradual descent onto your heels. Breathe in to elongate the spine and harmonize the energy centers, then breathe out to gently bend forward over your legs, allowing the point between your eyebrows to make contact with the ground before you. This will effectively enhance and stabilize the energetic foundation of your third eye. The act of grounding this location also resembles the act of sealing a bottle, symbolizing the prevention of any further negative energy from entering.

- The practice of Padangusthasana, commonly known as Big Toe Stretch, is a yogic posture that not only enhances grounding but also provides a delightful sensation for the body. Assume a seated position with your legs extended apart and ensure that your spine remains upright and in proper alignment. Take a deep inhalation to direct focus towards your third eye, and then proceed to exhale while leaning forward towards the right side. Curl your fingers around your large toe, ensuring that your forehead rests gently against your leg. Once you have completed the exercise, proceed to perform it on the opposite side in order to achieve symmetrical stretching of your legs.

Exercises for the coronal energy center

The crown chakra represents the pinnacle of energy within the human body, and therefore demands tender nurturing and reverence. It is imperative, within the context of this meditation, to visualise in one's mental perception the manifestation of energy converging at this juncture. Envision an illuminating glow emanating from your third chakra while reciting its sacred mantra, the syllable OM. Kindly maintain a focused awareness of your breath at all times, ensuring it remains deep and steady.

Another effective technique that can be employed is practicing alternate nostril breathing, which facilitates the balanced circulation of energy at the crown. Please utilize your index finger to occlude the left nostril and proceed to inhale deeply through the right nostril, maintaining this pattern for a count of five breaths. Next, proceed to transfer your finger to the right nostril and inhale through the left nostril for an additional duration of five breaths. You may choose to engage in this alternative breathing technique for approximately five minutes, or until a sense of revitalization is experienced in the crown region. Similarly to meditation, direct your attention towards the crown area while engaging in this practice, referred to as Nadi Shodhana in Sanskrit.

The asanas encompassing the crown chakra are designed to invigorate the upward circulation of energy towards the pinnacle of the cranium.

- Salamba Sirsasana, also known as the Headstand, is a highly beneficial yoga pose. Assuming a position where your head makes contact with the floor, even without attempting a complete headstand (which may appear daunting), can facilitate the expansion of your crown chakra. Assume a wide stance and maintain an upright posture. While expelling air from your lungs, gradually descend your upper body towards the ground and shift forward to a point where your head can make contact with the floor. Create a triangular shape by placing your head and two flat palms on the ground in order to provide stability during your headstand. Gradually increase the pressure exerted on your head and hands while initiating an upward thrust from the surface. In due course, you will acquire the ability to elevate them overhead, transitioning into a headstand position.

- Adho Mukha Svanasana, known as Downward Facing Dog, encourages the extension of your spine while simultaneously fostering the flow of energy towards the crown chakra. In this particular position, the formation of your body assumes the shape of an inverted V. Your hands exhibit a full contact with the floor, while the soles of your feet manifest a complete level of contact with the floor as well. Your hip placement is adjusted to a suitable position, allowing for a gentle curvature of the spine.

Yoga plays a pivotal role in the process of restoring and harmonizing the chakras. There exists a myriad of yoga variations, all of which possess advantageous qualities. One may discover that one particular activity engenders a greater sense of equilibrium or personal enjoyment. In such an instance, it is advisable to cultivate and integrate this practice into one's daily routine. An advisable course of action for individuals who are new to yoga is to attend a beginner's class offered by a yoga group. This could be practiced in Hatha Yoga, a style known for its energetic flow, or Kundalini Yoga, a discipline focused on the use of sound. These categories are characterized by simplicity in acquisition while retaining an element of complexity, providing ample opportunities for advancement. It is also possible to engage in individual practice within the confines of your own room; nevertheless, it is advisable to initially acquire some knowledge from an instructor.

Each individual yoga posture featured in this book can be seamlessly integrated into a comprehensive yoga regimen or sequence, or alternatively, can be performed independently. There are several assertions suggesting that engaging in a daily practice of twenty to thirty minutes can expedite the healing process of one's chakras. While there may be validity to your statement, it is crucial to exercise caution. Engaging in excessive activities simultaneously can potentially result in an overwhelming effect, leading to potential harm to the well-being of your chakras. The aforementioned statement applies equally to the postures (asanas) themselves. Please exercise caution and prioritize your safety when engaging in any physical activity. If you are unfamiliar with the practice of yoga, it is advisable to avoid attempting advanced poses such as headstands. Doing so could potentially lead to disappointment, injury, and pose a hindrance to your progress. Yoga centers around your individual experience, therefore it is imperative to attentively heed the cues and messages your body conveys. If one is attentive, they will be aware of their own limits, recognizing the appropriate boundaries to adhere to and the subsequent yoga postures that should be practiced.

An alternative approach to facilitating the healing of your chakras involves utilizing crystals and therapeutic minerals. These stones possess an inherent energy that facilitates harmonization of one's personal energy. An effective guideline to follow entails utilizing stones that mirror the hues associated with the respective chakras, particularly when seeking to address the healing of a particular energy center. Certain renowned crystals have been scientifically verified to possess potent abilities in harmonizing the various chakras, clear quartz being a notable example. Clear quartz is readily available and affordable, rendering it a viable option for addressing disruptions within one's spiritual or physical well-being, regardless of the circumstances.

In regards to the root, chakra incorporates minerals such as tiger's eye or lava rocks. Red and brownstones are well-suited for balancing this particular chakra. The sacral chakra requires the presence of citrine, which is an orange-hued gemstone. Colorful coral works well. To restore the warrior chakra, one may employ yellow topaz or other gemstones of a yellow hue. The heart chakra seeks the beneficial energies of rose quartz, a blush-toned quartz variety renowned for its protective properties and suitability for incorporating into one's daily routines. To bring harmony to the throat chakra, it is advised to employ blue turquoise and sapphire gemstones, whereas the third eye chakra can be balanced by incorporating amethyst gemstones. For optimal alignment of the crown chakra, it is recommended to utilize clear or purple gemstones.

These are just a limited selection of stones to begin with; however, there exist numerous additional ones that will assist you. It would be advisable to consider wearing crystals, stones, minerals, and gems in the form of jewelry positioned near your neck or in proximity to the specific chakra that requires harmonization. You have the ability to position these items throughout your residence, inside your vehicle, or even at your professional establishment—any location where you frequently dwell stands to gain from the presence of harmonized energy, thereby attracting positive energy towards your chakras.

Insufficient emphasis cannot be placed on the efficacy of self-conduction in achieving chakra equilibrium. This entails merely conducting oneself in a manner that is supportive of the well-being of chakras, by embodying love, kindness, and compassion in all aspects of one's endeavors. Cultivate empathy by adopting the perspective of others, adopt a composed demeanor when experiencing anger, and abstain from reacting impulsively. Engage in open and honest communication about your emotions to prevent internalizing them (detriments to your chakras), and strive to display a positive demeanor whenever feasible. Attempt to release negative emotions and resentment. In case you encounter difficulties with this matter, engaging in the practice of yoga and meditation would be beneficial for you. You will discover the process of releasing the burden of loss and traumatic experiences, as well as extending forgiveness towards those who have caused you harm, to be an integral facet of your personal healing journey. Exercise caution and deliberate thought prior to taking action, and you will discover that you are inclined to make more prudent choices, resulting in significant positive effects on your chakras.

To cultivate a sound mind, it is imperative to maintain physical well-being. If one does not currently possess a daily regimen of physical activity, it is imperative to establish and incorporate such routine. This may appear to be an insurmountable task, particularly for individuals who are unaccustomed to engaging in physical activity. However, it is imperative. When the body enters a state of stasis, a similar condition befalls the mind and spirit. There is a decrease in the flow of energy within your chakras, resulting in a state of diminished vitality and underutilization. Toxins accumulate within your physical and spiritual being, and engaging in physical activity is the sole means to eliminate a portion of them. Furthermore, physical activity serves as an exceptional means of alleviating stress. It enhances your physical appearance and boosts your self-esteem, greatly influencing your overall spiritual well-being.

www.ingramcontent.com/pod-product-compliance
Lightning Source LLC
Chambersburg PA
CBHW050414120526
44590CB00015B/1959